tricks of the trade

From Best Intentions to Best In Show

REVISED EDITION

by Pat Hastings
with Erin Ann Rouse

DOGFOLK
ENTERPRISES

Aloha, Oregon

Tricks of the Trade: From Best Intentions to Best In Show
Revised Edition

Copyright ©2005 by Dogfolk Enterprises

First edition copyright ©2000 by Dogfolk Enterprises
First edition, second printing, 2002

Printed and bound in the United States of America. All rights reserved.

Published by Dogfolk Enterprises, 17195 SW Division, Aloha, Oregon 97007, 503-642-3585

Cover and graphic design by Bridget Backus McBride, Spotted Dog Creative
Front cover photo by Peggy T. Rouse
Back cover photos by Meg Callea and Peggy T. Rouse
Interior photos (unless specified otherwise) by Carl Lindemaier, Animal World Studios,
  Peggy T. Rouse and Libby Workman
Illustrations by Grace Harper
Computer illustrations by Karen McClelland

Printed by Bridgetown Printing, Portland, Oregon

Visit Dogfolk Enterprises online at www.dogfolk.com

ISBN 0-9678414-3-7

For E. R. "Bob" Hastings
1924 — 2002

*Without you, I would not be offering the pearls
among these pages to others.
You taught me always to put the dog first,
to cherish my wonderment of puppies,
and to stay true to myself and my beliefs.*

*With Love and Gratitude,
Pat*

preface

This book is based on a seminar I gave to dog clubs and other organizations within the Fancy for 15 years. The seminar was based on the combined experiences of two lifetimes spent in dogs—mine and my late husband's, E.R. "Bob" Hastings. It was geared toward the experienced dog person—breeder, exhibitor, and judge alike. However, on many occasions, these individuals were accompanied to the seminar by a spouse or friend who loved dogs but was uninvolved in the sport. Of these people, many came up to me at the end of the second day and expressed enthusiasm for what they gained. Vets who attended expressed their appreciation for being able to extend their knowledge beyond medicine to the dog itself.

When I decided to retire the seminar, I began reviewing the notes I had accumulated over 15 years and decided that the book needed to be revised to include as much of the seminar information as possible. Both the original and revised editions of this book were written primarily for the benefit of people directly involved in the sport of purebred dogs. However, all of us who love, interact, or share our lives with dogs can learn from experience—our own or someone else's. With that in mind, I invite all dog lovers to peruse this book and glean from it ideas and approaches that might enrich your relationship with your favorite dogs. Whether we are breeders, exhibitors, or just people who get a kick out of dogs, these pages may have something useful to offer each and all.

I am reminded that everyone who is active in the sport began as a pet owner. Whether we move on to Conformation shows, Obedience work, Field Trials, Agility competitions, or simply neighborhood pet parties, our first best motive is love: for the eyes that watch our every move (especially at mealtime), for the tail that wags in overwhelming joy at our return, for the unconditional affection our dogs give without a moment's hesitation.

Dogs build their sense of security on routine and clarity of rules, but they thrive on a sense of purpose and challenge. They love being couch potatoes, but they are almost always ready for an Olympian sprint across a beach or field. They may shy away from a balloon or windup toy, but they are fearless if their loved ones are threatened. We have so much to offer each other. For our part, the offering comes from how much we are willing to learn for the benefit and welfare of our dogs.

I wish to extend my appreciation to all of those who came before us; to all of the authors from whom we have learned so much; to all of the veterinarians who have been willing to teach us, as well as learn from us; to the judges who have shared their insights and perceptions with us over so many years; and to our fellow handlers, exhibitors, and breeders who have always been willing to help make us better dog people.

More specifically, I extend my gratitude to Erin, for making me write this book (with her help); my brother, Tom, who told me I couldn't do it; my brother, Peter, who knows me better than that; and my late brother, Fred, who made us all better people; to Mike Billings, Edd and Irene Bivin, Ed Bracey, Dr. Lisa Branford, Marj Brooks, and Dr. Dan Buchwald; to Anne Rogers Clark, Lee Ann Clark, Dr. Jodi Engle, Herman and Judy Fellton, Ed Gilbert, and Charlie Hamilton; to Lanny and Sabin Hamilton, Bill Holbrook, Ron and Laurie Lane, Dr. Jim Layman, and Karen McClelland; to Dr. Del Orchard, Dean Partridge, Lang Skarda, and the late Dr. Barclay Slocum; to my daughters, Audrey and Laurie Smay and my granddaughter Taisha Rae; to Cathy Spears, Patti Strand, Diane Vasey, Bob Waters, Seymour Weiss and Libby Workman. Each of you has helped to breathe life into this book.

And finally I am grateful to those who contributed to the quality of the revised edition: Erin (of course), Linda Arndt, Dr. Randi Brannan, Phantom Lake Borzois, Kathy Corbett, Greg and Liana Craven, Dawn Danner, Dr. Shereen Farber, Viviana Flores, Grace Harper, Rebecca Jones, Thesese Price, Dave Redpath, Peggy T. Rouse, Ron Scott, Dr. Bianca Shaw, Terry and Mary Strom, Karen Walker, Sally A. Waller, Marty Young and

Northwest Doberman Rescue.

And to Dr. Hal Engle, who eventually is going to get tired of all my questions–thanks, Hal.

Mary Jane Hunt wrote: "The moment of victory is much too short to live for that and nothing else." To all of you who have given me the benefit of your support, encouragement, experience and companionship, I thank you for making my life so plentiful.

The quotes leading off each of the chapters to follow are some of my favorites from *The Road to Success Is Always Under Construction* (Larry Wall and Kathleen Russell) and *Think Big: A Think Collection* (Dr. Robert Anthony).

table of contents

*Where you come from isn't as important
as where you are going.*

---

introduction

I have worked and lived with dogs all of my adult life, as did my late husband, Bob. We started as owners, got involved in breeding and became professional handlers. Before we took on the awesome responsibility of living with and showing other people's dogs, we apprenticed for many years with professionals who taught us proper care, animal husbandry and canine physiology.

Bob was an American Kennel Club (AKC) representative for five years, advising judges and exhibitors on show rules and regulations. We were both involved in Obedience; Bob was part owner of an Obedience school for a time. Early on, I was very active in 4-H dog events, helping youngsters to become good dog people. And throughout our careers, we were both active in kennel clubs, holding offices and working on committees. We chaired all-breed shows and national-specialty shows, and both of us became AKC judges. At this writing, I am an AKC judge for the Non-Sporting, Herding and Working groups, Junior Showmanship and Best In Show.

We have taken many of the routes that one can take with dogs. We were very honored and fortunate to have shown great dogs. In our careers, we won over 250 Best In Shows, and we won Best In Shows from all groups. Between us, we bred 28 different breeds and we bred in every group. Even when we only bred a litter or two of a certain breed, we did so to learn more about the breed, because there is no better way to learn what a breed is all about than to have puppies, watch them grow up and follow them through their lives.

I do not claim to be an expert on any particular aspect of dogs; I have no degrees connected with the dog world. This book is simply a compilation of what Bob and I learned over the years and what I continue to learn.

Your knowledge is only as broad as your exposure, and because of who we were and what we did, we had the opportunity to have a worldwide exposure that the average dog exhibitor never has a chance to experience. Knowledge is wasted if it is not shared, so between our mentoring activities, my seminar and presentations, this book and future educational projects, I am trying to give something back to the dog world–a world that has given me so much.

AKC is concentrating on judges' education and doing a fine job of it. However, AKC judges can only judge what exhibitors show, so I feel education needs to start with breeders. (At this writing, I am pleased to note that AKC is developing a Breeders Department.) In the bygone days, there were large breeding kennels, complete with managers and private handlers. These kennels housed large numbers of brood bitches that could be bred to a considerable variety of studs in order to produce the strongest lines. This environment also developed dog people with a thorough knowledge of animal husbandry, defined best as the careful management of animals. And it made for skilled mentors from whom we could learn dogs from the ground up.

In today's world, there are very few large kennels and professional dog people; therefore, too many people are breeding dogs without fundamental dog knowledge.

A prime example is found in advertising. If breeders, exhibitors, handlers and judges universally were well versed in structure and movement to the extent of having a full working knowledge of both, we would not see an abundance of poorly built dogs advertised–dogs that are winning as well as being used in breeding programs.

I sat down with several current dog magazines one day and ended up with booklets of advertising photos that display dogs with serious structural and movement faults. Would owners, breeders and handlers with a working knowledge of structural quality purposely publish such photos? Maybe some of these dogs are well structured and the photography is simply uncomplimentary. What does it matter whether the photo is poor or the quality of the dog is poor if the visual presentation offers an incorrect or improper representation of the breed?

Everybody complains about "politics" in the sport of purebred dogs. However, it is more the perception of politics that is at work than actual politics. As a professional handler, I knew there wasn't much politicking; as a judge, I have come to realize there is even less of it than I supposed as a handler.

The fundamental truth is that dog show judging is very subjective. What counts most (and what many exhibitors overlook) is the whole package. The best dog does not necessarily have the best chance of winning. The best package has the best chance, and the package has to include a quality dog that has been properly raised, conditioned, trained, groomed and handled.

An AKC judge has 2.4 minutes to judge a dog. This includes paperwork, ribbons and pictures. With this in mind, it is perhaps easier to understand why the best dog may not win the day. The judge simply does not have time to see past poor grooming, insufficient training or a lackluster presentation to recognize what might be there under different circumstances.

In order to have the edge, you need a quality package. Winning is a matter of learning how to put the whole package together. That's what this book is all about. It's all hard work—there are no shortcuts. However, if you continue to do what you have always done, you'll continue to get the results you have always gotten. If you aren't where you want to be in the sport, try another approach—what have you got to lose? Don't be afraid to ask questions: There are no dumb questions when you're working to increase your knowledge base. When we stop asking questions, we stop learning. Remember, education is the learning of all the things you didn't know that you didn't know.

What I will be discussing in this book are commonsense practices that have worked for us. They are not necessarily the only things that work, but they are approaches and, if you will, "tricks" with which we have had the best results.

As professional handlers, we went to an average of 100 shows per year and showed 15 to 20 dogs per show. This gave us the opportunity to have our hands on thousands of dogs. The ideas discussed in this book worked with almost all of the dogs we handled.

Be fair to yourself. Don't begin reading with the thought that your current approach is wrong. I simply offer some additional information to consider. And always keep this in mind: Your dog is your dog. Don't let anyone—be it your breeder, your vet, your handler, your best friend or me—talk you into doing anything with or for your dog that you're uncomfortable doing.

There is no substitute for good breeding. However, it is entirely possible to ruin even the best-bred dog; it happens to the best-intentioned of us all. My hope is that this book will give you a greater edge on how to care for and enhance a show-worthy dog, and possibly even how to enjoy your dogs more.

We all start in the same place, knowing absolutely nothing. We don't have to be in dogs very long before we think we know everything. As soon as we admit that such is probably not the case, we can begin again. From that point on, we find we are open to learning for the rest of our lives.

If you can't find the time to do it right the first time,
when are you going to find the time to do it over?

first things first

Showing dogs is one of the only sports in the world where everyone is on a level playing field. It makes no difference if you are an amateur or a professional, male or female, old or young. It does not matter what you do for a living or where you live. Everyone in dogs can accomplish exactly what they want to accomplish, as long as they are willing to do the necessary learning and work. And don't delude yourself with the excuse that it takes a fortune to succeed. If you are breeding and showing great dogs, the money will find you.

Although it may not cost big money to succeed in dogs, it does cost money. If you cannot afford proper equipment for your show dogs, you probably shouldn't be showing dogs. The array of equipment and supplies on the market is limitless. You don't have to buy it all; just learn how to spend your money on the things you really need. It is possible to succeed without spending a fortune.

There are three pieces of equipment that we feel are the most important tools you will own for all aspects of your life with show dogs:

1. One or several leather kennel leads.
2. A top-of-the-line, quality grooming table.
3. A sturdy grooming arm.

With these three tools, quality and durability are of paramount importance.

Figure 1-01: Kennel lead

Figure 1-02: Kennel lead in use

KENNEL LEADS

Leather kennel leads are difficult to find, but no serious dog fancier involved in anything other than Toy breeds should be without one at every door and in every vehicle you own. It is the safest way to move a dog from one place to another—with something secure around its neck and your hand attached to it.

Because it is sometimes troublesome or inconvenient to put a collar and lead on or attach a lead to a collar, we can become very lax about doing it with each car ride or walk to the mailbox. A collar by itself is generally insufficient, as is leading a dog by its hair or ear. A leather kennel lead is easy and reduces unforeseen risks.

GROOMING TABLES

There are many types of grooming tables on the market, so make sure to do some homework before you buy. It is always better to purchase a table on sight instead of through a supply catalog, since pictures can be very deceiving. You need to see what you are getting—feel the weight (a consideration if you are going to cart it around to shows); check the welding and the edging. Make sure nothing is loose and no parts can develop instability with usage. Check with your hand to ensure there are no rough edges on which you or your dog can be injured.

For a quality table that will last a long time, the most important factors to consider are the height of the cross-member of the legs and the width between the vertical braces. The closer to the ground the beam is and the wider the braces, the more stable the structure. Moreover, the less motion in

Figure 1-03: Low crossbeam   Figure 1-04: High crossbeam   Figure 1-05: Wishbone legs

a table, the longer it lasts—the lower the center of gravity, the less motion.

Each time there is movement in the structure, the welding is compromised; thus, if the cross-member is high and the width between the vertical braces is narrow, the table will wear out much quicker.

The shape of the table legs increases in importance with the size of the dog being worked. One common table leg used today is the wishbone shape. Although a table with wishbone legs is perfectly safe for small breeds, it can be a hazard for large breeds. If a large dog attempts to jump up from the side onto this kind of table or moves toward the side or edge while on it, the table could easily tip sideways. Whether the legs are square or round tubes seems to be irrelevant.

Another important quality to look for in a table is a nonskid surface. Keep in mind that the table is a tool not only for grooming but for teaching and molding. All show dogs should be taught confidence on a table; behavior patterns should be addressed on a table. However, any motion or slickness to the surface on which a dog is being worked can potentially harm that dog's show career.

If the rubberized surface of a table is grooved with the length of the surface, it will not provide the dog sufficient traction. Make sure the grooves run with the width of the surface.

There is a variety of table surfaces on the market, so make sure the surface of the table you are considering is as skidproof as possible. Also, avoid using tables with carpeted surfaces. Carpet offers inadequate traction, can create static in the dog's coat and may disguise spills and accidents that can undo all of your hard work in a grooming session.

Figure 1-06: Correctly grooved surface

Figure 1-07: Incorrectly grooved surface

Figure 1-08: Grooming arm with appendage in place

Figure 1-09: Grooming arm with appendage folded

GROOMING ARMS

For a good grooming arm, look for a solid structure with as little motion as possible once it is in place, high or low. There are grooming arms available that are sturdy and hinged. This reduces the chance of bending or snapping, and you can move the overhang appendage of the arm out of the way, which simplifies matters if you are using the table for activities other than grooming.

With these three tools, take as few chances as possible. Buy quality, even if it means you have to spend a little more than anticipated. The return on your investment is worth it.

Experience is a wonderful thing. It enables you
to recognize a mistake when you make it again.

puppy evaluations

Mortality, by its very nature, suggests that all living things have in common a mix of strengths and weaknesses. It follows, then, that the primary objective shared by all conscientious dog breeders is to improve the quality of their respective breeds. The goal is to breed for a perfect blend of:

❖ Type.
❖ Genetic integrity.
❖ Good temperament.
❖ Structural soundness.

Everything that you read and hear today about show dogs stresses type. Type is certainly the most important thing in the show ring; after all, type is what makes a specific breed. Type, however, must be taken within the context of the basics that comprise structural soundness. You have to have both type and structure to come up with a quality dog. Whether you are breeding or buying, it is of paramount importance to learn how to evaluate the structural quality of puppies.

Evaluating for structural soundness is a piece of the formula for success. You have to put it together with breed type, coat, colors, the status of your breeding program, etc. However, the formula is fundamentally flawed if it excludes the inborn composition of a dog's physical structure.

In this undertaking, there is no such thing as a "pick of the litter." Frankly, the pick of a poor-quality litter is still poor quality. Although "pick of the litter" is a common phrase among dog people, we'd be wise to eliminate it from our mind-set and our vocabulary. What's required is to evaluate each puppy in relation to a standard of structural excellence and the breed standard, rather than evaluating it in relation to its littermates.

To assess breed type in puppies, study your breed standard carefully, bearing in mind what you need in your breeding program to improve type in your lines. To assess physical structure, the more advantages you have, the better—everything from a knowledge of canine anatomy to an understanding of genetics. And, again, know your breed standard well.

My late husband and I used the process discussed in this chapter for several years and were able to track the accuracy of our process through documentation and follow-up evaluations. Currently, I evaluate an average of 300 litters per year and results continue to amaze me. See what it can do for you and for your breeding program.

PROCESS PARAMETERS

As breeders, my husband and I made the same kinds of mistakes over the years that every breeder makes. We've all kept puppies we shouldn't have. We've all sold puppies we later wish we'd kept. And we've all placed some puppies with families whose lifestyles were incompatible with the puppies' capabilities. Throughout our involvement in breeding programs, we kept asking ourselves: What are we missing?

In our search for answers, we met with Dr. Hal Engle, head of the anatomy department at Oregon State University's School of Veterinary Medicine. The exchange of ideas at that meeting started us on a journey plotted by more and more questions.

Our research led us from one vet school to another, from general-practice vets to orthopedic surgeons, from research facilities to engineers. Each resource provided a piece of the puzzle; our challenge was to put that puzzle together. We took up the challenge and developed the evaluation process discussed herein.

The process parameters we recommend are as follows:

1. For structure, evaluate puppies only at eight weeks, give or take three days either way. This is crucial. Before eight weeks, soft tissue is not sufficiently developed to hold the bone structure in place, which means you are able to "mold" a puppy into the picture you want to see.

As all bones grow at different rates, it is important to realize that the proportion of bone growth is as similar to the adult structure at eight weeks as it's ever going to be during the growth of the puppy. Therefore, what you see and, more importantly, what you feel at eight weeks is what the puppy will grow into as an adult dog.

This applies to all breeds across the board. The only exceptions we have found are premature puppies and puppies that have not had a good start. We've never had consistent results evaluating these two exceptions.

2. Evaluate the whole litter. Keep detailed records on every puppy in every litter you evaluate. You can then make the best possible breeding choices later on. It makes no difference if you recognize breed disqualifications or obvious pets among the puppies. Evaluate them all.

Understand that the real benefit of evaluating litters is education. The more breeders learn, the more their breeds benefit.

3. Keep a written record of each evaluation. Always record the results of each evaluation in writing. Then, when developing your breeding program, you will have not only pedigrees to consider but also the added advantage of written evaluation results. The more information you have, the better informed your breeding plans will be.

4. Select an objective grading system. I use a point system of 1 to 5: "5" being the best; "3" being an average dog of its breed that you see currently in the show ring; and "1" being the least desirable. However, you may find it easier to use a broader scale in order to better differentiate between notable attributes and mediocrity or worse. I suggest a scale of 1 to 9: "9" being the best; "5" being an average dog of its breed; and "1" being the least desirable.

The reason for an objective grading system is to maintain focus on quality. It's so much easier to get where you want to be in dogs if you breed quality. Subjective grading encourages you to overlook structural weaknesses in favor of the puppy that captures your heart. Maybe its personality is just too cute, or maybe it possesses a single outstanding element you'd hoped the breeding would produce. But what about the puppy as a whole?

If you don't work to eliminate structural weaknesses from your breeding program, you will stand still and so will your breed. Produce quality dogs, and then concentrate on type, coat, colors and preferences.

The structural evaluation process is used to improve a breeding program, not to proclaim the arrival of the next record-breaking show dog. Bearing that in mind, any puppy that has any structural piece evaluated lower than average should be excluded from your breeding program. These puppies usually have structural issues that can impact the quality of their lives as they age, especially if they are often engaged in activities that over-tax their already compromised physical capabilities.

If the puppies you evaluate do not possess better structural quality and type than what you already have, don't keep any of them. If you want to be a top breeder, trying to represent a mediocre dog as great is self-defeating. Try again, and keep your sights on quality.

5. Evaluate puppies at a place completely unfamiliar to them. Puppies are too comfortable where they live. They need to be evaluated in a place where they've never been. Another room in your house doesn't count, because it all smells the same to puppies.

6. Have someone unfamiliar to the puppies handle them for the evaluation. The worst person to evaluate a litter for its structural quality is the breeder. It certainly can be done, but it's just human nature to try to make our "favorite" puppies look the best. The breeder may find that partiality rules his or her evaluation findings. Basically, let someone working with a different breed handle the pups for the evaluation of your litters, and you handle their pups for their litter evaluations. That way, everyone learns. And it behooves us all to learn beyond our own breeds.

7. Evaluate puppies in a mirror. This is essential for an objective review. Look at the picture in the mirror, not at the animal in your hands. A mirror provides distance; it gives you the opportunity to step away from the puppy without ever having to step away from the puppy.

8. Let your fingertips be your best set of eyes. Your fingertips relay a great deal more information to your brain than your hands or your eyes do.

The most accurate view of a puppy's bone structure and tissue strength comes through tactile contact. Feel for skeletal formation, muscle mass and motion as allowed by ligamentation. It's important to remember never to push past the point of resistance when feeling for motion.

Use "soft hands," fingertips and gentle motions. You will be amazed how much you can perceive this way.

9. Be consistent in your evaluation steps. It is all too easy to let personal inclinations color the way we evaluate a litter. In order to achieve the greatest possible accuracy, every puppy must be evaluated the same way and with as much objectivity as possible.

Attachments and preferences only hinder the benefits of the process. Handle each puppy the same way. Use the same procedure each time with each puppy. Concentrate on getting every puppy in as natural a position as possible.

Evaluate the entire litter, one puppy at a time. Resist the temptation to discuss your findings as you go. Once you have finished your evaluations and have recorded all of the grading, plus specific comments on temperament, testicles, mouths, balance or whatever, determine and write down an overall score for each puppy.

THEN—*and this is very important*—go over the litter a second time to discuss each puppy. This time, take the puppies in reverse order, starting with the least-quality and working your way up to the best-quality puppy. This method will help you develop an eye for what is correct.

To evaluate for grading, we suggest the following procedure:

First, check **temperament**. To evaluate a puppy's temperament, turn it gently over on its back and

Figure 2-01: Correct hold for evaluating temperament

cradle it in your arms and against your body. You want to give the puppy every opportunity to feel it's securely held, so that what you see is the puppy's genetic temperament traits, not a fear of falling. (While the puppy is cradled in my arms for the temperament evaluation, I check eyes for color.)

Figure 2-02: Correct hold for suspended position

Next, look at the whole puppy in a **suspended position**. You need to position the puppy in such a way that it hangs free, without bearing any weight, and is completely relaxed. Pick a puppy up only on the bone structure of the skull/jaw and between the rear legs—without touching the testicles, if it's a male. In this way, you won't influence anything the puppy's body does naturally. This is perhaps the most difficult part of the process to learn but also one of the most important elements to a successful evaluation. Remember to hold the puppy as far back on the skull/jaw as possible. Do not lift the puppy if there is any resistance.

If you pick puppies up properly, they will relax and allow it. If you pick them up improperly, they either grab for your arm or fight you. Keep trying until you learn how to do this without stressing the puppy. If the puppy resists what you're doing, believe it. Return the puppy to its original position on the table, slide its feet backwards on the table a couple of times, and then return the puppy to its original position. When you feel the puppy relax, only then do you pick it up again. Remember to be soft, slow and gentle. It is all too easy to teach puppies that they do not want this done if you try to force them into compliance. If done correctly, however, there will be no resistance and no negative experience for the puppy.

Bear in mind that the way a dog carries its head and neck is determined by the quality of its shoulders. Generally, then, the better the shoulders, the easier puppies are to pick up in this fashion. If your technique is correct and the puppy still fights you, chances are that the puppy's structure is the problem.

Figure 2-03: Correct front hold for suspending

Figure 2-04: Correct rear hold for suspending

A well-structured puppy with proper tissue will hang in a very nearly stacked position. If that isn't what you see, there is a structural cause, and you need to determine what that cause is.

Figure 2-05: Standing position

Figure 2-06: Suspended position

Next, look at the whole puppy in a **standing position** on the table. Just try to make the puppies stand in a comfortable position. If they fidget, pick them up in the same fashion as you would for a suspended position, and run their feet along the table surface a couple of times. Puppies dislike the feel of a surface moving beneath their feet. Once you scrape their feet lightly across the table, they're usually so glad the table is no longer moving that they hold still.

After the puppy is standing comfortably and balanced on all four legs, the first thing you look at is the **overall balance**. Resist the temptation to "fix" the puppy. Just stack it in as natural a position as possible. Remember, the shape of the puppy at eight weeks is the shape it will grow back into as an adult.

Check the puppy's **proportions**, in accordance with your breed standard. In other words, check the height in relation to the length, and the depth of the body in relation to the height of the leg. Make sure you are following your breed standard, as some standards require the dog to be longer than it is tall, to have a sloping topline and so forth.

Figure 2-07: Check height at shoulder

Figure 2-08: In relation to length of body

With the puppy comfortably stacked, look at the **whole picture**. Learn to look for correct balance by visualizing three simple lines that apply to most breeds:

1. Visualize a line along the entire topline. The head—jaw and all—should be above that line.

Figure 2-09: Check depth of body

Figure 2-10: In relation to height of leg

2. Visualize a line up the front legs, perpendicular with the ground. The entire head and neck of the puppy should be in front of that line. Remember, legs weren't designed to hold up the head; they were designed to hold up the body.

3. Visualize dropping a plumb line from the point of the buttocks to the ground. The plumb should land at the tips of the toes.

Practice these visualizations with every dog you encounter. Pretty soon, those lines will come easily to your mind's eye when evaluating puppies. Once they do, you will be able to look at the whole picture and immediately detect such significant structural weaknesses as a short neck or poorly placed front or rear assembly. When you start going over each piece of the puppy, you can search out the cause of these weaknesses, but looking at the whole picture with

Figure 2-11: Visualization of whole picture

your imaginary lines in place will tell you the weaknesses are there.

After assessing the puppy as a whole, methodically go over each piece in the same order for each puppy. I go over a puppy in the following order:

1. Testicles.
2. Head.
3. Neck (length, shape, arch).
4. Shoulders (angle, fit, width, smoothness).
5. Prosternum (surface, placement).
6. Upper arm (angle, proportion).
7. Elbows (motion).
8. Front piece.
9. Depth of chest and shape of ribs.
10. Underline.
11. Length of the ribcage and loin.
12. Hock angle and height.
13. Rear assembly proportions.
14. Fit of the knees.
15. Placement of the feet.
16. Shape of the pelvis.
17. Balance of muscle mass on the legs.
18. Hock stability.
19. Topline.
20. Croup.
21. Tailset.
22. Bite.
23. Occlusion.

Last, but most certainly not least, evaluate the **nutritional effects** on structure. Position the puppy facing the mirror. Make sure the front legs are

Figure 2-12: Front legs suspended to show true structure

Figure 2-13: When legs bear weight they show the nutritional effects

hanging free, without bearing any weight, and the puppy is completely relaxed. This shows you the true structure of the front legs. Gently lower the front feet back onto the table. If the front legs lose whatever soundness was seen while suspended, the problem usually is nutritional, not structural.

One thing I ask all breeders whose litters I evaluate is: What are you feeding the puppies? Almost all name-brand dog foods are top-quality products. However, we in the world of show dogs have a tendency to feed more than our puppies can utilize. Because of this, premium puppy foods that contain additional nutrients can allow the growth rate of bones to increase. Since there is no way to increase the growth rate of tissue, rapid bone growth can create structural problems.

Try to feed puppies according to their lifestyle. If they are confined to relatively small areas, they need only standard nutrients. The more activity and freedom they have, the more they are capable of handling additional nutrients.

Structural problems caused by nutrition are usually correctable by changing to a quality adult maintenance food. However, the change must be made before the growth plates close. After that, structural problems caused by inappropriate nutrition are irreversible.

Finally, give all puppies the best possible chance at an objective evaluation. Work to keep them calm during the procedure.

Some people swing puppies in the air to calm them or act as though they were dropping them off the end of the table. However, both of these techniques generally produce the opposite results.

I use cheese during evaluations—not as bait, but simply as a way to keep puppies' minds off what I'm doing. Cheese is easy on their stomachs and keeps their interest. You don't want to use anything so enticing that you lose control.

Remember they're babies, not adult show dogs. You want to be as soft and gentle with them as possible.

A PREFACE TO DECISION MAKING

Before we start talking about ideal structure and issues that deviate from it, we need to address how to keep structural weaknesses in perspective. As we noted at the start of this chapter, all living things have in common a mix of strengths and weaknesses. Perfection in a dog doesn't exist. We can—and should—strive for ideal structure, but every dog will have some flaws. That's life. So how do we keep structural faults in perspective?

First we need to learn as much as possible about structure and how it impacts the dog. Then we need to go back to the history of each breed in order to understand its original purpose. Any structural weakness that impedes the dog's ability to fulfill that purpose also diminishes its breed type. Purpose is an essential component of type, whether the breed still does what it was bred to do or not. We are the guardians of these breeds, and maintaining proper type is one of our most fundamental responsibilities.

That brings us right back to structure. As mentioned earlier, proper shoulders create proper neck and head carriage. Without proper shoulders, a dog loses efficiency of movement. This means less to, say, a Schipperke (bred to be a barge dog) than it does to a hunting dog, be it a Hound or Gundog. With improper shoulders, a hunting dog is incapable of working all day.

By the same token, high shoulders allow a harness to rub against bone, which creates bone bruises. This is not an issue for Lhasa Apsos (bred to be indoor watchdogs), but it is a significant issue for sled dogs. A water retriever with a ewe neck cannot swim effectively. A dog that does repetitive jumps or works on rough terrain will break down faster if it has a lack of prosternum or loose elbows. A herring gut limits stamina, which is a serious impediment to Sighthounds (bred to chase down game or race).

Such issues are balancing points to decisions based on structural evaluation findings. A long loin or weak union makes a dog more susceptible to back injuries, which is a serious issue for Pembroke or Cardigan Welsh Corgis (bred to drove cattle). Similarly, cow hocks or barrel hocks are a serious issue for herding breeds because they cause destabilization of the hind quarters, which puts these dogs in harm's way when working livestock.

Slipped hocks affect many things, one of which is temperament. Toy dogs are bred to be companions. Cranky, potentially threatening Toy dogs are many times in pain due to compensation for slipped hocks.

The list is endless, but it is our responsibility as breeders to learn the importance of structure as it pertains to the purpose of our specific breeds and do everything possible to strive for the best structure possible, at the very least within the context of purpose. This goal benefits both the breed and each puppy from our breeding programs.

EVALUATING FOR DECISIONS

In some respects, breeding dogs is a roll of the dice. Breed the best you have to the best you can, and you may still end up disappointed, having to let go of a whole litter and begin again. This is an inherent risk taken by even the most experienced dog breeders.

At the same time, making accurate decisions about each puppy's future can be equally difficult, unless you're measuring against a standard of excellence that includes a good temperament and structural soundness.

Temperament

The temperament we are all looking for shows itself when the puppy is lying on its back in the arms of a stranger in a new environment. The puppy should be totally relaxed and look its bearer right in the eye (how long a puppy will look at you is very breed specific). These are signs of a basically secure, self-confident puppy, which is what we'd like to see in all of our puppies. However, other temperament traits may be present, and we are wise to know how to recognize them so that we can do the best job of successfully placing puppies.

1. Insecurity. A puppy that holds on is usually an insecure puppy. Insecurity manifests itself later as a dog more comfortable and at ease at home than elsewhere. For example, all of us have heard someone at one time or another say: "If the judge could come to my house, this dog would be finished." Such a dog is usually insecure. Keep in mind that it is perfectly normal for a puppy to grab hold when being turned over on its back. The puppies that don't let go once safely cradled are the ones you want to be particularly careful about when selecting homes for them.

2. Fear. A fearful puppy will open its eyes wide when you tip it down head first a bit in your arms. You will be able to see the whites of its eyes and can actually see the fear. A fearful puppy may grow up with an exaggerated startle response and a greater fear of things. Many times, they are also sound-sensitive. Encourage the adopting family to work toward building the puppy's self-confidence instead of deferring to its fearful tendencies.

3. Aggression. An aggressive puppy will not let you hold it on its back, no matter how much you try to get it to relax. Be cautious about placing an aggressive puppy in a family with children or with an inexperienced dog person. A puppy that would bite a person to get its way could come back to bite you in your reputation.

4. Detachment. A puppy that will not meet your eyes can be a real challenge. These puppies usually are very independent and will march to a different drummer. Everything they do is done on their terms. The trick is to make them think your terms are theirs. Note that this trait can be present along with any other temperament trait.

When you identify any of these traits, socializing and exposure to a variety of positive experiences can help mask them, but the genetic causes of such traits will remain intact. Remember that you can modify behavior but you cannot change temperament. Therefore, write down the traits you identify so that you will be aware of them if you use a puppy with any of these traits in your breeding program later on.

Because of this, we need to understand the significance of evaluating temperaments and learn how to identify temperament traits so that we always place puppies with temperament issues in the most appropriate homes.

Head

Evaluating the head is a very confusing proposition. It is a task best performed by the breeder, because the breeder should have a strong sense of what a good head is for the breed, including eye and ear placement. When you look at the head of an eight-week-old puppy, if it's what you're looking for in an adult, then you need to find out if it's going to stay that way.

1. Head shape. In determining how the head will develop, you first want to evaluate the ridge or zygomatic arch (ie, cheekbone) that runs between the eye and the ear, as well as the areas below and above that ridge. If the surface of the ridge is flat, and the areas below and above the ridge are fairly flush with it, then the back skull is most likely going to grow in proportion to what you are looking at. If the lateral surface is not flat, the back skull will most likely broaden out of proportion. The actual curve of the zygomatic arch is very breed specific. For instance, a Collie or a Fox Terrier has very little curve. An Akita or a Bulldog has a pronounced curve.

Figure 2-14: Zygomatic arch from side

Figure 2-15: Zygomatic arch from front

The curvature of the ridge between the eye and the ear is made up of two bones. The strength of the muscle attachment on the head is what keeps those two bones from separating. The separation of those two bones allows the back skull to broaden. If there is a significant indentation above the ridge, the head will usually develop a dome shape.

If your evaluation indicates that the back skull will remain in proportion, ear placement and the shape and placement of the eye will remain proportionally the same as well. If the back skull broadens out of proportion, the shape and position of the eyes and the position of the ears may change as a result.

2. Muzzle. In evaluating the head, the next feature to check for is a round, pellet-like formation on the skull bone at the inside corner of the eye. It will feel like a small pearl. This round formation is part of the growth plate that controls the width of the muzzle as it grows. If that tiny ball is present, normally the muzzle will grow forward in proportion to what you're looking at. If it is absent, and you feel a small indentation instead of a tiny ball, the muzzle probably will narrow.

Figure 2-16: Simulated growth plate at inside corner of eye

3. Bite and occlusion. When looking at the mouth, the bite needs to be what your breed standard calls for, but don't stop there. Check the placement of all four canines, and check for proper occlusion on the sides.

The side teeth fit together like cogs of a wheel or teeth on a pair of pinking shears. If they're misaligned, the mouth can change well into adulthood. This is one of the reasons why good mouths can go bad.

If there appears to be a problem with the alignment of the canines, talk to a dental vet about interceptive orthodontics—a perfectly legal option, when dealing with puppy teeth. According to one report, interceptive orthodontics is effective in 50 percent of all cases.

Finally, make sure all of the necessary puppy teeth are present and accounted for. Get in the habit of counting teeth; be aware of teeth when making your breeding plans (for adult tooth chart, see Chapter 6, p 110).

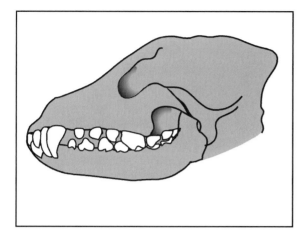

Figure 2-17: Proper occlusion (adult mouth)

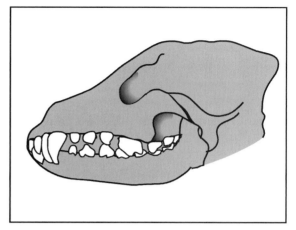

Figure 2-18: Improper occlusion (adult mouth)

Figure 2-19: Occlusion of puppy teeth

Good breeding practices have to begin with an applied knowledge of the basics, and teeth are as basic to a dog as they are to any land mammal, including humans.

Neck

In most breeds, the neck is of paramount importance in detecting front assembly problems. If you were to draw a line along the puppy's topline, its head should be well above that line. If it isn't, the puppy has a short neck, which almost always indicates something is not quite right with the front.

The most common cause of a short neck is straight shoulders. All dogs have seven vertebrae in their necks; however, a straight shoulder can cause an xray to show only five or six. This is because the shoulder blade itself is actually hiding one or more of the vertebrae.

Another cause is a poorly placed front assembly. Place your left hand under the chest and with your index finger and thumb, squeeze the elbows

Figure 2-20: Good neck

Figure 2-21: Short neck

together just until you feel resistance. If the elbows come together, the placement of the front assembly is the problem.

In such a case, the reason you can move the elbows is because the upper arm is in front of the ribcage instead of alongside the ribcage. This causes a sloppy upper arm movement—like an

Figure 2-22: Good front assembly

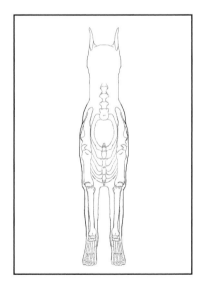

Figure 2-23: Front too far forward

egg beater—instead of a good, strong forward action.

What matters is that a dog with a short neck—whatever the cause—will almost always have less reach, because a dog usually can only reach to the end of its nose, so the shorter the neck, the shorter the reach. (Remember

Figure 2-24: Good reach

Figure 2-25: Short reach

"reach" is where the front foot hits the ground when gaiting, not how far forward the front leg stretches.)

The appearance of a short neck can also be caused by a **ewe neck**. One of the ways a puppy or dog compensates for this structural issue is to tuck its head into its body, thus giving the appearance of a short neck. A ewe neck can be caused by two very different problems. The first and most common is improper ligamentation, which allows the neck to bend both directions. Tucking the head in alleviates the stress of supporting the weight of the

Figure 2-26: Good neck

Figure 2-27: Ewe neck from improper ligamentation

Figure 2-28: Ewe neck when tipped back

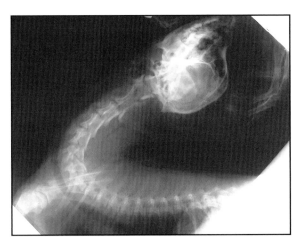

Figure 2-29: Xray of ewe neck

Figure 2-30: Correct neck

Figure 2-31: Ewe neck from dropped vertebrae

skull on the weakened neck. Another way dogs compensate for weak ligamentation is to pull the head and neck back and up, thus creating a straighter column of support for the skull.

The second cause of a ewe neck is dropped vertebrae at the withers. This causes the base of the neck to jut forward, putting the neck in front of the body and the front legs too far under the body. This creates the illusion of front-heaviness, as if the dog could easily fall forward onto its nose. No matter what the cause, if you can gently tip a dog's head back past vertical, it has a ewe neck.

The three most common indications of a ewe neck are:

1. Convex curve on the front side of the neck.
2. A lack of arch at the crest of the neck.
3. An angle instead of a curve where the neck meets the withers.

Figure 2-32: Correct neck

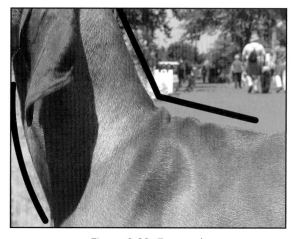

Figure 2-33: Ewe neck

Front Assembly

Bones have to be balanced to work in unison. Equidistance means the dog will be able to move its front assembly muscles properly. With this in mind, most breeds should have the appearance of approximately the same length from the prosternum and the notch near the point of the shoulder to the top of the blade as from the prosternum and the notch to the bump in front of the elbow.

Figure 2-34: Front assembly equidistance

1. Shoulders. The shoulder blade should sit at the angle described in your breed standard, which, in most cases, is referred to as "well laid back" or "45 degrees."

Few people have the ability to look at an angle and know its degree. Most of us can see a horizontal or vertical line or a 90-degree angle, like where a wall meets a ceiling. However, eyeing the difference between 40-, 45- and 50-degree angles is beyond most of us. Fortunately, most of us have a built-in tool for measuring the angles that count on our puppies—our hand. For example, put your left hand up; straighten and stiffen the fingers, and then straighten and stiffen your thumb perpendicular to your hand. You have just created a 90-degree angle.

Figure 2-35: Hand at 90-degree angle

Now, put your left hand up; straighten and stiffen your fingers, but relax your thumb. Without moving any fingers or your thumb, turn your hand until your thumb is horizontal with the ground. The angle between your thumb and index fin-

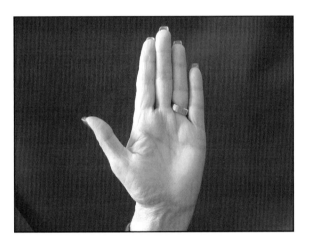

Figure 2-36: Hand at 45-degree angle

ger is an approximate 45-degree angle. When you are looking at a puppy's shoulder, put the point at which the line of your thumb meets the line of your hand on the notch near the shoulder, with your thumb horizontal to the ground. This would be a 45-degree layback. To determine how far off ideal the shoulder actually is, align the line of your fingers with the spine of the scapula (the ridge that runs up the center of the shoulder blade) and see how far off horizontal the line of your thumb is.

Figure 2-37: Hand showing 45-degree shoulder angle on dog

Figure 2-38: Hand showing true shoulder angle on dog

Although there is an enormous amount of controversy regarding the feasibility of 45-degree shoulder angles on dogs, do not allow this controversy to become an excuse for not breeding the best you can. Remember, the straighter the shoulder, the shorter the reach.

The shoulder blades should fit smoothly and blend onto the ribcage. In most breeds, you should not be able to see the shoulders, and you should hardly be able to feel them. They should never be the highest point of the dog. The top of the shoulder blade should always lie along the ribs slightly below the high points of the spine. A scapula that is higher than the high points of the spine causes the dog to carry its neck upright, giving the illusion of a long neck. In truth, the neck is shorter than it appears (see figures on p 48).

If they fit properly, they will usually have the proper space between the tips. If the tips are too far apart, the dog will move wide up front. If the tips are too close together, the dog's ability to lower its head will be restricted. And if a dog cannot eat out of a pan on the floor without lying down, how is it going to do the job for which it was originally bred, such as retrieve, hunt or track?

2. Upper arm. Although you constantly hear in the show world about short upper arms, we see relatively few of them in our puppy

Figure 2-39: Good shoulder

Figure 2-40: High shoulder

evaluations. Short upper arms appear to be quite breed specific, whereas straight upper arms can be found in almost all breeds. However, it should be noted that the straighter an upper arm is, the shorter it will be. Both of these problems can be found with or without correct shoulders.

3. Elbows. With your left hand over the puppy's shoulder blades, push gently to the side. If this motion "pops" the elbow out, the dog will throw its elbows as an adult. Consequently, the dog may also toe in up front. This "popping" or elbowing out is the result of improper ligamentation.

4. Prosternum. The sternum is the bone underneath the chest to which the ribs are attached. The prosternum is the forward end of that bone that protrudes on the forechest.

The puppy should have a prosternum that you can almost hold onto with your fingers. Since a good prosternum surface is necessary for proper muscle attachment, which links the upper arm to the ribcage, a lack of prosternum may result in a very loose forward motion similar to what you see when the upper arm is attached too far forward.

The prosternum is at the same level as the notch where the upper arm and the shoulder blade meet. On a dog that has a properly proportioned front assembly, the prosternum aligns with the center of the ribcage; in other words, if you draw a horizontal line through the middle of the ribcage from the rear forward, it will end at the prosternum. If the prosternum is low on the body, the puppy has a short upper arm. If the prosternum is high on the body, the puppy's upper arm is too long and/or the scapula is too short.

Depth of Chest

The depth of the chest at eight weeks should be what it is supposed to be as an adult. If the bottom of the chest is flat, the puppy will usually retain the depth. If it feels curved (as if it comes to a point underneath) instead of flat, it usually will outgrow the depth you are feeling.

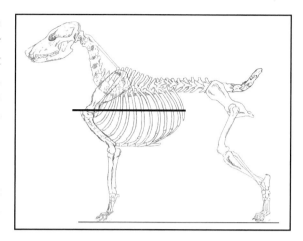

Figure 2-41: Point of prosternum aligns with center of ribcage

A chest that is too far below the elbow is just as faulty as a chest that is too shallow. The elbow must be capable of clearing the flat part of the ribcage. It should not run into the curve of the ribs.

Finally, put your hand on the chest between the front legs. If your fingers reach an angle under the ribs, this usually is indicative of a herring gut. The depth of the ribs should extend to the ninth rib. If it does not, the

Figure 2-42: Good depth of chest

Figure 2-43: Herring gut

resulting problem can affect the amount of stamina the dog has as an adult, as Mother Nature will not allow any part of the heart or lungs to protrude outside of the ribcage. The more extreme the underline, the less lung capacity and stamina the dog will have.

Length of Loin

The puppy's loin is measured from where the last rib comes off of the spine. The distance from the last rib to the pelvis should be much shorter than the distance from the last rib to the shoulder.

If the puppy's loin is too long, the area between the last rib and the pelvis has no support. In an otherwise well-built dog, this usually is not much of an issue while the dog is in its prime. However, a long loin may exaggerate the physical challenges imposed by other existing structural issues that affect the topline. In either case, a long loin can have an adverse effect on a dog as it ages and always makes a dog more susceptible to back problems.

A loin that's too short poses its own set of challenges and problems. The dog's ability to bend sideways resides in the loin. Some Terriers have gotten so short-backed that they don't have a loin left, so they are incapable of turning in or backing out of a hole. You have to get a shovel to dig them out after they get stuck. Too short of a loin is an issue for Sighthounds as well, since it hinders the dog's ability to maintain a double-suspended gallop.

Rear Assembly

As stated earlier, bones have to be balanced to work in unison. Equidistance means the dog will be able to move its rear assembly muscles properly.

Insofar as the rear assembly is concerned, the length between the point of the buttocks and the kneecap – or patella – should be approximately the same length as between the kneecap and the hock.

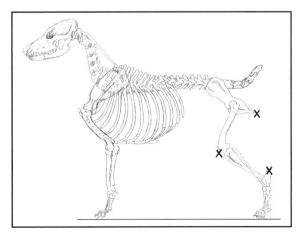

Figure 2-44: Rear assembly equidistance

If the lower thigh is too long, it moves the stifle joint farther up the leg, so at eight weeks, the leg may look quite straight. It will also take longer for the rear assembly to develop proper strength; however, what strength does develop may not last as the dog ages. A long lower thigh also creates added stress on the joints.

1. Rear angulation. Breed standards vary enormously when it comes to rear angulation. From the Chow Chow, expected to have a stifle with little angulation and an almost straight hock joint, to the Dachshund, expected to have right angles, and everything in between.

Just remember that at eight weeks, a puppy must have proper length of leg and appropriate angles for its breed. Be sure you evaluate this piece in relation to your breed standard.

Rear assembly balance for most breeds is the same. Imagine dropping a plumb line down from the point of the buttocks to the ground. On a well-balanced, well-structured rear assembly, the plumb would drop right at the toes. This is the balance point required for proper movement.

If the rear legs are too long and the feet fall far behind the plumb line, the puppy has the most commonly seen form of sickle hocks. As the puppy moves its feet forward for balance, the hocks appear to be bent in the form of a sickle.

True sickle hocks, where the rear pasterns actually curve, are very rare. In over 22,000 eight-week-old puppies, we have seen only seven with true sickle hocks. When the bones of the rear pastern are actually curved, the dog will be unable to flex the joint backwards. All of the other reasons why a dog does not extend behind are compensations for a structural issue of one kind or another, such as rear legs that are too long and/or a croup and tailset that are too low for the breed.

When the plumb line drops behind the tips of the toes, the rear legs are too short. This is usually the result of shortness in both the upper and lower thighs—the bone between the pelvis and knee being the upper thigh and the bone between the knee and

Figure 2-45: Proper rear assembly

Figure 2-46: Sickle hocks—
rear legs too long

Figure 2-47: Sickle hocks—
legs too long, foot at line

Figure 2-48: Sickle hocks—
curved rear pastern

Figure 2-49: Short rear legs

the hock being the lower thigh. Rear legs that are too short cause a much straighter rear assembly and create a compensatory column of support that can flatten the pelvis (reduces the angle of the pelvis so that it is more horizontal), which in turn can result in a high rear. Short rear legs can also contribute to a "gay" tail carriage.

2. Pelvis. All dogs from behind should be shaped like an inverted U. If the puppy you are evaluating is shaped like an inverted V, it may have a narrow pelvis and will move narrow behind (see figures on p 53).

If the puppy is a bitch, think carefully about whether you want to keep her in your breeding program, because a narrow pelvis increases the chance that you'll be paying for more caesarian sections, as well as potentially losing puppies due to prolonged deliveries and delays in electing to perform caesarian sections.

Generally speaking, the majority of breeds—with the notable exception of Bulldogs—should never be narrower across the rear than they are across the shoulders.

3. Knees. In most breeds, the kneecap—or patella—should flow toward the inside of the front leg on the same side. If

Figure 2-50: U-shaped pelvis

Figure 2-51: V-shaped pelvis

you evaluate a puppy whose knees point out, that puppy will be much more susceptible to injuries, such as patella problems or torn cruciate ligaments. The general lack of normal weight bearing can result in added stress on the stifle and other joints in the rear assembly. The dog looses its ability to bear weight properly on the joint. Consequently, the dog will compensate in one of three ways: It will move wide behind; it will move with either a swishy or sashaying motion; or it will move its rear legs in either a bicycling fashion or an up-and-down, piston-like action.

Luxating patellas—or slipped kneecaps—are not something we check for. You're much better off leaving that determination to your vet.

4. Placement of feet. When you're evaluating the rear, one of the things you look at is which way the rear feet point when you pick up the rear slightly and drop it. If the feet point out, the dog will stand as if it were cow-hocked, even if the dog is not cow-hocked. However, make sure the feet are not pointing out as a result of some other structural issue, such as improperly aligned knees. Also, check your breed standard, because a few standards allow for rear feet to point out.

While moving, a barrel-, spread- or open-hocked dog will toe in behind with hocks out. Both barrel hocks and cow hocks are usually caused

Figure 2-52: Cow hocks
(heavier muscle on inside)

Figure 2-53: Barrel hocks
(heavier muscle on outside)

Figure 2-54: Good hocks
(balanced muscle)

by an imbalance of muscle mass on the inside or outside of the leg. All muscles need to be balanced, in order to minimize the dog's susceptibility to injury, since stability is created by opposing force.

5. Hocks. Hocks are the cornerstone of the rear assembly. The rear pastern should be perpendicular to the ground, and the hock joint itself should have no forward or side motion to it.

The shorter or more let down a hock is, the more endurance and strength it will have. At eight weeks, the hock should be no more than one-third the total height of the dog's rear.

A potentially serious hock problem that is far too commonly seen is **slipped hocks**, also referred to as "double-jointed" or "popping" hocks. In the evaluation, the puppy with slipped hocks generally will not hold its rear in a stacked position. It will constantly be moving a rear leg forward.

A slipped hock is when the joint itself bends the wrong direction. It hyperextends or collapses forward. A slipped hock is different from short rear legs, which can create straight stifles and hock joints. This is often referred to as "peg legs" or "post-legged."

Figure 2-55: Good hocks

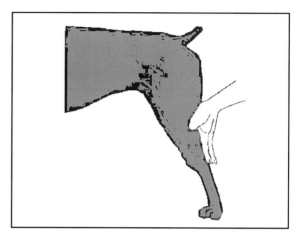

Figure 2-56: Slipped hocks

Slipped hocks are caused by a weakness in the tissue, not in the bone. The reason the puppy moves its leg or legs forward is because the hock joint will not collapse with the legs farther underneath the body. If a puppy has slipped hocks at eight weeks, it almost always has slipped hocks the rest of its life, no matter how it learns to compensate. But how many other problems does that compensation cause?

Hip dysplasia is thought to have a substantial genetic compo-

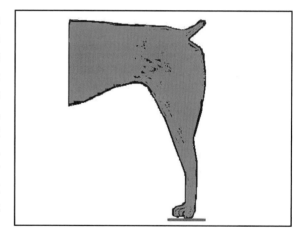

Figure 2-57: Straight stifle and post-legged hock

nent. However, if a dog has a predisposition to hip problems and a joint beneath the hip wears out, the next joint up the line is going to take on more of the burden of balance and movement. When the hock wears out, the knee compensates. When the knee wears out, the hip compensates. Common sense tells us that all structures are composed of balance and compensation. Therefore, be aware that slipped hocks can cause the puppy serious problems later on, if the weakness is dismissed.

Figure 2-58: Skeleton of hock

Figure 2-59: Skeleton of hock falling forward

Topline

When you are looking at the topline of a puppy or dog, remember that there is a slight dip where the bony projections on top of the vertebrae change direction. This is the hole that the late Dr. Quinten Laham called "the knick," and it is normal. A topline problem is very rarely created by the spine. One exception is known as a "weak union" in the spine, which means there is too much space between the vertebrae that joins the loin to the hips. The body compensates for a weak union by building a roll of muscle across the topline. Some people mistake this roll for fat. Keep in mind that where there is a problem, there is a cause.

A bad topline is almost always a compensation issue. Therefore, to really understand the topline, we need to return to the front and rear assemblies.

1. Front assembly effect. If there is softness or there are holes in the topline, they usually stem from some problem in the front assembly. For example, if a puppy's front is too far forward, there will usually be a hole directly behind the shoulder blades. If a dog has straight shoulders or straight upper arms, it will usually have a soft topline. Wrinkles over the shoulders usually indicate straight or wide shoulder blades.

2. Rear assembly effect. If there is a roach to the topline where there shouldn't be one, it usually stems from some problem in the rear assembly. Many dogs with slipped hocks will have roached toplines. In order to keep the pressure off their legs, they try to carry more weight in their backs. You can see the same effect in older dogs that have developed arthritis in their rear assemblies.

Croup and Tailset

If in your evaluation of a puppy you find that the croup and tailset are bad, you need to know that they'll probably never get better. Even if they're correct, however, they can change for the worse over the next two years of the puppy's life.

The determining factors are the three vertebrae between the hip and the tailset. These vertebrae fuse together, and they are the last bones in the body to calcify.

The croup and tailset are dependent not only on the attitude of the dog but also on the rear structure. The weaker the structure is behind, or the fewer chances a dog has to run in wide-open spaces, the greater your chances of losing a proper croup and tailset.

On an eight-week-old puppy, you want to see a tailset that's appropriate, with respect to your breed standard. With a tail that is supposed to be carried up, you want to see a "shelf" or a protrusion of the buttocks behind the base of the tail. Exerting a slight forward pressure at the base of the tail should produce a 90-degree angle from the topline to the tailset.

With a tail that isn't suppose to be carried up, you want the base of the tail to be in a straight line down the rear. Also, at the intersection of the topline and the tail, you want a curve—never an angle.

If the tailset or the rear is too high, check the point of the buttocks. These bones should feel like they are parallel with the ground. If they angle up, the puppy could have a tipped pelvis. In a bitch, this could contribute to whelping problems.

General Presentation

We do not evaluate movement in eight-week-old puppies. They are going to move however their brains tell them to, and brains aren't always in full communication with legs at eight weeks of age, especially in male puppies. In addition, many movement issues are actually weight-bearing issues, so they do not show in youngsters.

It is, however, very important to watch puppies on the ground, because the way puppies use and carry their bodies–in other words, the way they naturally present themselves–generally stays with them throughout their lives.

The puppy on the ground who seems to say, "Just look at me: I'm fabulous," will almost always keep that kind of attitude. The one who walks around with its head tucked and shoulders slumped will usually grow up with that kind of attitude.

The most difficult thing for any animal to do is to stand still. The same is true for people. In order for a dog to be comfortable standing still, it has to be well made and balanced. So the puppy that stands proud without fidgeting is probably the most well-structured puppy in the litter.

The more structurally imbalanced a puppy is, the more it's in motion. Additionally, the best-built puppies usually trot. The ones that usually bunny-hop generally have the greater number of structural weaknesses.

Substance

The size and substance of an eight-week-old puppy mean very little. The smallest puppy in the litter can turn out to be the largest dog and vice versa. However, a puppy should weigh what you think it's going to weigh. In other words, when picking up a puppy, you shouldn't be surprised by the weight in your hands.

This has to do with bone density, and if bone density is out of balance with the rest of the puppy, the pup can grow up either spindly or clunky. Always be mindful of the fact that physical structure is all about balance and compensation.

CONCLUSION

The three most important reasons to evaluate litters of puppies are:

1. To determine whether there are structural issues. If there are structural problems, search out their causes. You can't fix anything in a breeding program until you know specifically what needs to be fixed. It does no good to look at a dog and say, "I don't like that rear," unless you know why you don't like it and what is needed to improve it in your next breeding.

2. To determine which puppies to keep in your breeding program. Use all elements of the formula for success. In other words, consider the results of your structural evaluations in conjunction with breed type, temperament, coat, colors, preferences and all other necessary elements.

3. To determine what kind of home is most suitable for each puppy that leaves you. It is up to us, as breeders, to make a match between a prospective buyer's lifestyle and the puppy whose structural qualities are most compatible.

There is no substitute for careful, responsible breeding. The only thing more important is to put the welfare of the puppies you breed before all else when making your decisions about where and how they will spend the rest of their lives.

Objective evaluations and careful record keeping can advance your breeding program, your breed, and possibly your show wins. But of course, there is more to winning than simply producing or buying a great puppy. Think whole package, whole package, whole package!

nutrition

FOOD FOR GROWING PUPPIES

When you consider that a puppy grows for 18 to 20 months and a child grows for 18 to 20 years, the speed at which damage can be done by improper puppy nutrition is staggering. Feeding a puppy improperly for one month is the equivalent of feeding a child improperly for one year. Thus, it is imperative to make sure your puppies are doing well on whatever you are feeding them. Just remember how quickly nutritional damage can occur, and once the growth plates close, nutritional damage is permanent.

Something we as consumers must rethink is the idea that more is better. Why would we want to feed our puppies more powerful nutrients than we feed our adult dogs? The overwhelming consumer response would be: "Because they're growing babies."

Let's think about that one for a moment. Do human babies receive more powerful nutrients than human adults? They start out on formula or breast milk, and then slowly move to strained, bland fruits and vegetables. They are hardly coaxed to gum down salads, steaks or multigrain dinner rolls. When was the last time you saw an infant chomp into a pepperoni pizza?

By the same token, do coyote pups or wolf cubs get the prime morsels of their parents' hunt? Certainly not. They either receive a regurgitated portion of the kill or morsels left over after the adults have eaten.

In a sense, we as consumers may have convinced the dog food companies that we want special food for our growing puppies and that we are willing to pay extra for it. And no one in Corporate America's right mind would ignore that kind of message. So it goes—we give the message that more is better, and we believe if something on the market costs more, it must be better. But what does this cycle mean for our puppies?

High-powered nutrients can enable bone to grow faster than it is meant to grow. However, the growth rate of tissue is unalterable. If a puppy receives more nutrients than it can utilize and those nutrients accelerate the growth rate of bones beyond the growth rate of tissue, the tissue can be weakened.

When I conduct puppy evaluations, I always pay close attention to how puppies are doing on the food they're being given. When I see nutritionally-based problems, my first recommendation is always to drop back one level in the quality of food the puppies are eating. This change almost always corrects the nutritional problems seen in the front legs and feet. (See Chapter 2, p 34-35.)

Try to feed puppies only what their systems and structures can use. If your puppies are running in the woods with their mother from five or six weeks on, they are spending enough energy to utilize almost any level of nutrients you choose to feed them. However, most of us raise our puppies in small yards, kennels, exercise pens and kitchens. In these situations, we need to be careful about what we feed.

Smaller breeds burn greater amounts of energy in confined spaces, so less damage is seen when these puppies are fed more high-powered nutrients. By the same token, however, the smaller the breed, the smaller the space provided, so

Figure 3-01: Puppy with poor structure due to nutrition (courtesy of Linda Arndt)

Figure 3-02: Same puppy after changing from a puppy food to an adult formula (courtesy of Linda Arndt)

nutritional damage is still possible.

My recommendation is always to feed a name-brand product. If you see any structural weaknesses that could be caused by what is being fed, switching to a lesser-power food (usually of the same brand) generally corrects the problem, as long as the growth plates have not yet closed. The younger the puppy is when this change is made, the faster the problem is corrected. As stated earlier, the nutritionally-based weakness becomes permanent once the growth plates have closed.

If you are feeding a quality, maintenance food to your adult dogs and they are in excellent condition, then that is usually what you can safely feed your puppies from day one.

Puppies should be given only their food; try not to offset the balance of this nutritional formula by adding other food items or supplements. The only supplement we suggest is Vitamin C. A past study out of Cornell University indicated that a Vitamin C supplement allows dogs to utilize more readily the available calcium in their bodies. There are numerous studies indicating that giving dogs a calcium supplement can cause more problems than it cures.

Supplementing with Vitamin C, which is water-soluble, will help only if help is needed. Vitamin C is part of the enzyme that links and strengthens collagen—a vital component of tendons, ligaments and joints. So even though Vitamin C supplementation may be controversial in some circles, its use poses little potential for harm.

DOG FOODS AND FEEDING

A friend of mine, Martin Coffman, DVM, offers a profound morsel of wisdom to all dog food buyers: "Read the dog, not the label." Always remember that the dog is the most important—and unique—element. Pay attention to your dogs' condition, weight, coat, physique, etc, and feed according to their individual needs. The ingredients listed on dog food packages may be in the food, but there is no way to know what the quality of those ingredients is or what percentage may be available for appropriate utilization.

Best rule of thumb: If what you're feeding works, don't let anyone talk you out of it. If it isn't working, try another food. Continuing with a food that isn't working well for your dogs then adding to it only means you are spending more money and effort than necessary. There are many good-quality foods and diets available. Use what works for your dogs.

How do you know your dog's food is working? If what you're feeding is working, your dog should:

- ❖ Be in good weight.
- ❖ Have tight feet.
- ❖ Have straight legs and pasterns (if called for in the breed standard).
- ❖ Have a full coat (no bare spots, not brittle or overly dry/oily) with a healthy sheen.
- ❖ Have clear, focused eyes.
- ❖ Have supple, smooth skin.
- ❖ Have no inflamed or irritated membranes (eg, ears, feet).
- ❖ Have a firm stool.
- ❖ Display an alert, animated attitude.

Have you ever wondered why 15 or so dog food companies all claim to have "proof" that their products are the best? Remember marketing does not a miracle dog food make. Stick to what works for you and your dogs.

Four significant points to consider are:

- ❖ Dogs stay in better condition if they are fed more than once a day.
- ❖ Dogs are better eaters if they eat warm food.
- ❖ Dogs are better eaters if they have more than one texture to their food.
- ❖ Most owners overfeed their dogs.

One more note: Be careful with supplementation. Webster defines supplement as "something added to make up for a lack." If dogs are missing something they need, a supplement can help. If your dogs are in good condition, a supplement can destroy that condition. As with puppies, give your dogs only what they need. As soon as you have fixed a problem, stop using whatever you used to fix it. And never use a supplement just because someone else does.

A HEALTHY WEIGHT

As far as weight condition, there are three elements to check for on your dog:

1. You should be able to feel all of the ribs with your hand, but your fingers should not fall between them.

2. You should be able to find the hip bones easily by touch, but they should not be visible (unless your breed standard calls for it).

3. When looking straight down on the topline of most breeds of dog, you should be able to see an indication of a waist.

An excellent habit to get into is to regularly look at your dogs before you feed them. If they're getting thin, feed them more. If they are getting fat, feed them less. Monitoring their weight day by day is so much easier than working to fix a weight problem once it has become all too obvious.

According to Dr. Janet Cook, a study done at UC Davis indicated that "lite" foods do not satisfy the daily requirements for a healthy, active animal. Therefore, they should only be regularly fed to severely overweight dogs. For dogs simply on the

Figure 3-03: Doberman Pinscher in good weight

Figure 3-04: Doberman Pinscher underweight

Figure 3-05: Doberman Pinscher overweight

hefty side, a lite food may not be an effective approach to dieting.

My husband and I found that the best way for us to take weight off of a dog was to feed it exactly what we had been feeding it all of its life and in the same bowl it had eaten from all its life. We just cut the food ration in half and make up the difference in volume with unsalted, unbuttered popcorn or rice cakes. This fills the dog's stomach without changing its regular food. Most dogs will lose weight rapidly on this regimen.

To put weight on a dog, first try feeding a lesser formula of the brand of food you feed. Sometimes, cutting down available nutrients makes it easier for dogs to utilize all of the food, and they can actually gain weight.

Second, try Lactinex, an inexpensive, live stomach enzyme product. It can be purchased at pharmacies and must be refrigerated. Add one tablet per 50 pounds of the dog's weight to the dog's food. Don't use more than one bottle. If Lactinex is going to work, one bottle's worth will get the stomach back on track. If there is relatively no change in the dog's weight after one bottle, it's not going to work, so stop using it. After all, there is no sense in using something that is ineffective.

Third, try a high-calorie nutrition drink such as Ensure. Just mix some in with the dog's food. It adds calories without adding volume. This is important because adding volume can cause loose stools, which in turn can cause the dog to lose additional weight.

Put an underweight dog on a good multivitamin, as any deficiency in zinc and Vitamin B can cause an impaired sense of smell and taste, which can contribute to weight loss.

Excessive weight on a dog is the more dangerous of the two conditions. An underweight dog may never have a great coat, since ingested nutrients are busy maintaining necessary body functions first, so there may be little left over to grow hair. But when a dog is overweight, its structure is compromised, especially if that structure is already less than sound and balanced. Discomfort from slipped hocks, hip dysplasia or arthritis is aggravated by excessive weight. Additionally, the dog's lungs, heart and circulatory system must work harder than they are meant to if the dog is obese. Also, canine athletes that are too heavy are at a much higher risk of injury.

Adults need less food than teenagers. This applies to your dog as well. Automatically cut back on a dog's quantity of food as it matures. Bear in mind, however, that dogs need high-quality animal protein in order to build and maintain proper muscle, so don't cut back on their protein intake. Along that same line, be careful about lamb diets. Lamb can be lacking in both L-carnitine and taurine, which are essential amino acids. A dog needs multiple proteins for appropriate muscle mass, and when considering muscle mass, remember that the heart is the biggest muscle in the body.

We have all been faced with a dog's pathetically pleading countenance when we fix a snack for ourselves. If the guilt is too much, remember that raw baby carrots make an excellent diet treat for dogs. Carrots are crunchy, contain no calories and get you off the hook.

Finally, a few brief thoughts on raw-food diets. I have seen many adult dogs that are on raw-food diets and many of them were in wonderful condition. However, the majority of 8-week-old puppies on raw-food diets that I have seen have had serious nutritionally-generated structural problems.

Here again, the raw-food diets seem to provide more powerful nutrients than most very young puppies can fully utilize. Also, if you are a proponent of raw-food diets, be aware of a parasite called Neospora Caninum, which may have some relation to canine encephalitis, myocarditis and paralysis.

You can obtain information from the internet (www.naturalholistic.com/handouts/neospora.htm), your vet or a board-certified canine nutritionist.

teaching a dog to learn

Dogs are not born with the instinctual ability to learn from humans. Learning is a taught behavior. The more words we teach our dogs, the larger their vocabulary becomes, and the more capable they are of learning. That is the first rule of thumb. The second rule of thumb is never do something for a dog that you can teach the dog to do for itself. Much like human children, puppies grow up more confident when they are taught to think for themselves. If you do everything for dogs, they will rely on you instead of learning to use their own brains.

INTERACTING WITH PUPPIES

The most important qualities you can instill in your puppies are self-confidence and an awareness of appropriate boundaries.

❖ **Teach instead of train.** Puppies are much like our own children; they will match their cunning against ours. Psychology is at work—it is wise not to underestimate this aspect in puppies or adult dogs. In order to teach puppies, we must think through each situation and pay attention to our behavior as well as theirs.

❖ **Never overdo anything with a puppy.** The second a puppy tells you "that's enough," believe it—that's enough. The most important thing to remember about your puppies is to let them be puppies.

❖ **Imprinting a pattern of behavior is one of the easiest ways to teach.** For example, when you start walking puppies and they're learning what the world is all about, as well as the vocabulary that goes along with it, save one toy that can only be played with during a walk. You can make a game out of them carrying this toy in their mouths on walks. They will learn to keep their heads up when they are on lead because of the toy they carry. Forming this type of habit creates a behavior pattern that will last a lifetime.

❖ **Every time you pick up a puppy for any reason—be it one from a litter of yours or a puppy you have purchased—put it on a grooming table.** The grooming table is all important because it is the most valuable conditioning and teaching tool you have.

Make sure your table is in a convenient place, and have it in front of a mirror, so you learn to look at the dog in the mirror, as opposed to looking directly at the dog. Each time you put the dog on a table, put it in a show stance. This is something a dog learns by doing—another case of imprinting a behavior pattern. And while you're at it, imprint a behavior pattern on yourself: Always look at the dog while you position it or do anything with it, and then look in the mirror to see the results. This is important to learn, because if you look in the mirror while you are doing something, you'll only confuse yourself.

As for the dog, just stack it on the table, without fanfare or instruction. Avoid setting up a "push comes to shove" interaction with the dog. For example, in order to avoid creating a counterforce from the dog when you're moving a leg, shift the weight off of the leg before moving it. This is a sensible concept to remember: All dogs oppose force, so avoid teaching your dogs to resist what you do. Start from the beginning of your puppies' lives to form the habit of "teaching" instead of "training."

Every time you do anything to that puppy—look at it, do its nails, check its mouth, clean its ears, weigh it, whatever—put it on the table in a show stance, keeping the head in a stacked position, moving legs in the same fashion you would in a show ring. In this way, you are imprinting on the puppy's mind what you expect of it. The more you place a puppy on a table in this manner, the more it will stand in a show position.

Do all of this in a teaching, instead of a training, fashion in order to continually set the puppy up for success rather than failure.

WORKING WITH DOGS

In order to have the best dogs, form a lifelong mind-set of teaching dogs instead of training them. This is a positive approach, both for the dog and for you, since teaching is a process of providing guidance toward appropriate behavior.

For example, when a dog acts tense or spooky, ignore it. By making an issue of a dog's negative behavior, you may inadvertently encourage that behavior. To develop good behavior in a dog, ignore the dog when it behaves badly (within reason) and reward it when it behaves well. That way, the dog learns for itself how to behave. Use common sense, though. Some behaviors must never be ignored, such as biting. All dogs must learn that biting is completely unacceptable (Schutzhund competition aside).

By the same token, if you focus on a problem, it may become a more serious problem. Find a way around the difficulty. This is a greater challenge for you than for the dog. An example would be a dog that shies when a judge is going over it. Perhaps the worst treatment for this problem is to make the dog endure people going over it, which sets it up to fail. Instead, take the dog to Agility classes, so it will focus on the fun of the activity rather than the people who are coming up to pet it.

❖ **The first rule of teaching is to help the dog understand you are the teacher.** This is accomplished with your voice, your body language and your control over all situations. All dogs need a pack leader—they need to know someone is in control. If you are not that someone, then the dog will take the position upon itself, whether it wants the job or not.

This can create an intolerable situation if you have a dog that wants to be in control—you may have your hands full, as the dog may grow to be uncontrollable or vicious. If the dog does not want to be in charge but feels it has no choice, then the dog may grow to be neurotic or so confused and uneasy as to make itself ill. Successful teaching begins with your resolve and your confidence. Dogs will learn from those in whom they can believe and take seriously.

For physical control, if you have control of a dog's head, you have control of the dog. This is imperative when teaching dogs, because if dogs think they can win, they will continue to fight you. If they know they cannot win, they stop fighting and settle down. And only when dogs are calm can they concentrate on learning.

There is no way to win arguments with dogs, so don't argue with them. If they know you are in charge, they will accept and respect your authority. Therefore, be willing to be the teacher; be the pack leader. It may require "tough love," but it is well worth the effort.

❖ **Help the dog build confidence by finding ways to teach it to think and do for itself.** For example, if the dog sidewinds in the ring, it may simply be resisting tension on its lead. Change the position of the collar, then walk the dog without tension on the lead and see what happens. All dogs need to believe they have a say in their lives. In order for a show dog to have a long career, they have to believe it was part their idea to want to be a show dog. Therefore, in order to prepare dogs to be show dogs, you have to be smarter than they are, or at least convince them that you are smarter. This can be a tricky proposition at times. The very best way to teach is to exercise your own best measure of common sense.

❖ **The reason a dog responds to a professional handler without a lot of pre-show practice is that good professional handlers know how to communicate what they want from the dogs.** Whenever you can make dogs think that changing their behavior is their idea, you are helping them become better show dogs. When a dog looks like it is showing itself, you are communicating well with your dog.

You cannot make dogs do things they don't want to do and expect them to look happy about it. You want to make being a show dog something they want to be. The more you practice with a dog, the more bored it becomes, hence the less of a show dog it wants to be.

However, if you work your dogs on a grooming table, they never seem to relate that to what's asked of them on the ground. First, you're not putting dogs in a submissive position when working them on a table. The more you work over the top of a dog on the floor, the more the dog gets the message that you want him or her to be submissive, and submissive dogs are less than great show dogs. Dogs must be taught how to stack and show like a show dog—they can't be forced into playing the part.

❖ **When it comes to lead work, I believe in lead-teaching, as opposed to lead-breaking, a show dog.** Dogs are lead-taught best on a buckle collar and a retractable or long lead. The reason for this is that the average dog owner has a tendency to jerk or pull on a short leash or show lead. A retractable or long lead teaches the person to talk more and yank less.

With puppies on lead, never make them go anywhere they don't want to go. Instead, carry them to where they don't want to be, and then let them walk back.

While your dogs or puppies are walking on lead, talk to them. Discuss things they're interested in—the fire hydrant or the flower beds you're passing. (Face it—your neighbors probably already think you're nuts, so it does no harm to add some fuel to the fire.) Talk to them constantly and positively. In this way, you condition them to respond to your voice.

❖ **If you have a dog that paces (moves both legs on the same side in the same direction), the easiest way to convince it that pacing doesn't pay is to find a hill on which to walk the dog.** Walk the dog along the side of the hill so that if it paces, it falls over. Two or three falls usually will convince the dog to gait correctly. If your dog spends part of its day in a kennel or run, placing PCV pipe (or something similar) through the wire in such a way that the dog has to step over it without being tempted to jump over it, will help break the habit of pacing. A dog is unable to pace and step over something at the same time (see Chapter 6, p 115).

❖ **The easiest way to start teaching dogs to do certain things is to teach them the words for what they're going to do.** If you know your dog is going to sit when you come up with a treat, teach it the word "sit" before it sits. If you know your dog is going to wag its tail when it sees something in particular, teach it to wag its tail. Use every opportunity to teach.

❖ **Handling classes may be one of the worst things you can do for a show prospect.** Handling classes are unbelievably important for exhibitors, but do your learning in such classes with a pet or a retired show dog–any canine but your show prospect. Show dogs can get incredibly bored at handling classes, and bored dogs make poor show dogs. Although dogs learn by repetition, the more you repeat something, the more dogs lose interest. Going through the motions of being a show dog for an hour at a time in class can easily destroy a show attitude. And attitude is part of the whole package. You need to learn how to handle a dog so it knows what you want of it in the show ring–that is the best use of handling classes. Until you learn how to teach and communicate with your show dogs, practice with a pet. Once you learn what you need to know, then you can become the teacher.

Dogs need socialization time, and handling classes can meet that need. However, if you take your show prospects to handling classes for socialization purposes, take them on equipment that is not used for show. If you take them on show equipment, you're going to go through the motions of making them look and act like a show dog. If you take them on a buckle collar and retractable or long lead, you can avoid that temptation more easily. This way, the dogs can get used to the situation on their terms instead of on your terms. Remember, they are there for socialization; you are there to learn.

Furthermore, you are responsible for your dog in any social setting, so pay close attention to interactions and reactions, and be on the lookout for canine rudeness (unacceptably crossing another dog's personal boundaries). If you're not paying attention, a retractable or long lead can get you and your dog into trouble.

❖ **If you have a dog that is shy or backs off or crouches in strange situations, always try to put that dog in a position to succeed.** Asking a dog to do something it is not yet capable of dealing with is inviting failure.

Instead, try to figure out a way around the problem. For example, take a grooming table to the handling class and put the dog on the table, where no one will be doing anything to frighten it or make it submissive. Let the dog decide that this situation is okay. (Make sure you pay the required class fee for this opportunity.) Use your grooming arm, and stay with the dog to make sure nothing happens; at the same time, don't protect it or do its thinking for it. Dogs need to learn they are responsible for themselves.

The dog should remain on the table until it has made the decision that all is well. It can then be worked on the ground. One dog may get comfortable with the situation in one class; another dog may take weeks of classes to develop the same comfort level. Each dog will take as long as it needs, so be patient.

❖ **Dogs dislike and respond negatively to being nagged (much like spouses and kids do).** Although we may not want to admit it, we know nagging is ultimately self-defeating. With this admission, do everything in your power to break yourself of this habit. Try to avoid using the word "no." It is very possibly the first word that both dogs and kids learn to ignore or tune out. Moreover, saying "no" robs the dog of initiative, as well as a willingness to keep trying.

❖ **According to many experts, almost everything that happens in people happens in dogs.** Most people think a dog is just a dog and you can do anything with or to it, but that is not true. Dogs are individuals. Dogs are right- or left-handed. Dogs can be slow or fast learners. There is mental retardation and insanity in some dogs. Some dogs are heterosexual; some dogs are homosexual. (This point, of course, begs the question, how can sexual preference be a conscious choice if some animals are gay?) Dogs can be far-sighted or near-sighted. A dog with depth-perception problems, for instance, can be uncomfortable on a table because of the height.

There is Down's syndrome in dogs, and it looks very much as it does in humans. There is hyperactivity in dogs, and vets sometimes use Ritalin to help alleviate symptoms. There is depression, and vets use Prozac. There is attention deficit disorder, as well as Alzheimer's.

Dogs face as broad a range of mental, emotional and physical challenges as we do. So you have to learn how to read dogs well enough to understand and accept that all dogs are not fixable; they're not all doable. Sometimes you have to cut your losses and move on. Also, all living things have a stress threshold that cannot be crossed. Try never to push beyond that point in your dogs.

❖ **The expression "it's okay" is one of the worst things you can say to a dog when it is behaving contrary to what you expect or need.** It is also one of the most difficult expressions to eliminate from our response file. Dogs reason differently from people; they cannot understand you are referring to the situation. They think they're being praised for their behavior.

For example, a dog fussing on the table hears "it's okay" and thinks it's okay to be fussy or in constant motion on the table. Generally, the most successful way to break the habit of saying "it's okay" is to work the dog with someone else around who can help you break the habit. Find a replacement expression, such as "you can do this" or "you can be brave," and use it often. After awhile, your mind will reach for the more effective expression before you have a chance to say "it's okay."

❖ **Once more with feeling: Don't do anything for a dog that you can teach the dog to do for itself.** A good example is placing a dog on a table. If you pick it up and put it on the table, you're depriving yourself and your dog of an opportunity to learn. Of course, small breeds are picked up and set on the table, but with larger breeds, teach the dogs to put their front feet on the end of the table, and then boost the rear and teach them to walk forward on the table while you are boosting.

Besides what this approach teaches, it has two advantages. First, it is less stress on your body to support a dog getting on a table versus picking up a big dog. Second, it is inadvisable to teach dogs to jump onto tables. Tables with a high center of gravity can tip if a large dog comes zooming up onto it from a bad angle. If your table is on a slick or non-level surface, accidents can happen. Also, a dog allowed to jump up on a table can cause problems in the show ring. Imagine how mortified you might be if you are running your dog around the ring and as you go by a table, the dog jumps on the table instead of continuing around the ring—it does happen.

The same thing applies to taking a dog off of the table. Let a dog leave a table only when you want it to get off. Support the dog underneath its loins with one hand and hold the collar or lead in your other hand, then teach the dog to get off.

Dogs are intelligent, intuitive, emotional beings. To treat them as less is a disservice to the dogs with which we live, work and compete. Moreover, discounting a dog's cognitive capabilities short-changes our own. Let's face it, teaching is a challenge to our wits and creativity, rewarding for both the person who accepts that challenge and the dog.

dog wherewithal

We all started in the sport of purebred dogs because we love dogs. However, sometimes we lose sight of that. It is particularly important, then, to take a moment every so often to remember that the dog is what's most important—the dog should take priority.

If you are spending so much time taking care of your dogs that you have no time to enjoy them, then maybe you have too many dogs. The right number of dogs is different for every single person, but for the sake (and well-being) of your animals, figure out what your limit is and stay within it.

Moreover, I firmly believe that every dog we own should be, in a manner of speaking, for sale. If someone comes along who can give one of my dogs a happier life and a home better suited to that particular dog, then the dog should have the right to go with that person, to that home.

With all that dogs offer us in their relatively short lifetimes, don't they deserve the best we can offer them?

PUPPIES AND LITTERS

❖ **Avoid keeping littermates, if at all possible.** Littermates tend to bond with each other, like twins. A dog that forms a strong bond with a littermate may not form strong bonds with humans. Another risk with littermates is that they may hate each other as they mature.

The most common risk is that one littermate will be overly

dominant, which may ruin the more submissive sibling. Is it worth the gamble that the best dog you ever bred or owned in your life ends up being an inadequate show dog because of one of these scenarios?

❖ **The structural changes puppies go through while they are growing up can drive you nuts if you keep looking at them.** One week, they will look great; the next week, they may look horrible; the next week, great again; the next week, so average as to be nondescript.

Make your decisions about puppies when they are eight weeks old, or at the age you deem appropriate, then put all decision-making on hold until the dogs are mature.

Too many breeders lean toward making decisions when the puppies look the way the breeders want them to look, which is oftentimes an unsuccessful approach. Remember, growing puppies can go into a good stage, then into a bad stage, and on and on, until they are structurally mature.

At the same time, it is unfair to our dogs to "grow out" litters and make our decisions when the puppies are older. I believe every puppy deserves its own home to grow up in and its own family with whom to bond. By the time puppies are 4, 6, 9 or 12 months old, they have left behind a developmental stage that is better experienced in its permanent home.

❖ **Color-marking puppies in each litter is an excellent idea.** However, be careful what you use. We always color-marked puppies with the strips of material used to make potholders. Bear in mind that Murphy's Law applies just as readily to breeding dogs and raising puppies as it does to other aspects of life: If something bad can happen, it will. Best to keep a close eye on your puppies, whatever material you decide to use for collars.

Color-marking (or color coding) provides the breeder with an alternative to nicknaming the puppies. If you call the puppies "pink" and "blue" and "green," they usually don't end up with birth names like "Tiny Tim" and "Big Bertha." You can be more objective about puppies if they don't have names; they are easier to part with and easier to evaluate. After all, how many of us have used a favorite name on a pup that didn't make the grade? I christened a puppy at birth with one of my favorite names; when I lost that puppy at 10 days old, I was too superstitious to ever again bestow that name on another puppy.

If you are going to color-mark puppies, do it from birth so that the mother thinks the "collar" is just part of the puppy. Color-marking also helps to ease puppies into the day when they need to wear real collars and begin lead work.

RAISING PUPPIES

❖ **When supplementing is required, bottle feeding is preferred over tubing.** The release of enzymes that enhance digestion is stimulated by suckling, and tube-feeding does not involve suckling.

❖ **It is imperative to keep a substantial supply of safe toys around for your puppies and to introduce them to toys when they are infants.** Toys (of varied weights and textures) that roll, squeak and smell interesting will draw their attention as soon as they have their tactile senses.

Early introduction to and rotation of toys imprints on the puppies what items are appropriate for wrestling and chewing. Without this imprinting activity, puppies are more likely to be indiscriminate in their destructive play.

A wonderful way for you to interact with your puppies is with a kid's old-time favorite—soap bubbles. Puppies love them, and you can monitor the development of their coordination, temperament and personality, as well as their position in the pecking order of the litter.

Another great toy is a good-quality car wash mitt, because puppies do not seem to be as capable of destroying it as effectively as they can destroy actual dog toys made of the same type of material. A word of caution: The cuff on a car wash mitt can be chewed to bits with very little effort. It's advisable to remove the cuff before tossing the mitt to enthusiastic puppies.

❖ **Environmental challenges at an early age aid in the development of the nervous system, which controls coordination.** The challenges need not be elaborate. Things to climb over, crawl under and go through can be enough. Crates taken apart and put on the ground, with the solid part up, can serve as both a den and a high place.

Kids' toys, such as Little Tykes® pre-school play pieces, hanging tennis balls and tires, large PCV pipes and beginning pieces of Agility equipment can help build confidence as well as coordination.

CARING FOR THE SHOW DOG

The reason top handlers (and I am talking about experienced professionals, not agents) do the majority of the winning, particularly on circuits and at clusters, is because their dogs are usually well rested, in good weight and feeling good physically and mentally. They are eating, drinking and eliminating as they should; they are not stressed from the heat. Owner-handlers' dogs are typically none of the above. This has nothing to do with politics; it has to do with the fact that most top handlers know how to take proper care of dogs and most owners do not. Let's look at what handlers do and why.

Conditioning

This is one area in which a professional handler has a real edge, since part of the handler's reputation is based on the condition of the dogs in his or her care. Most owner-handlers are unaware of everything that goes into prime conditioning.

1. If you are a breeder or involved in the world of show dogs, the first step in conditioning is to select a good veterinarian. This is quite a trick, because really good vets for dog-show people are few and far between.

One problem with vets is us. We expect our vets to be dog people, but they are medical professionals, educated to treat diseases. For example, there is almost no mention in any veterinary class that I know of about whelping puppies. If your vet is not a dog breeder, he or she may never have seen a litter of puppies born. Most students of veterinary medicine are given almost no education on nutrition. Many vets only know what salesmen have told them about dog food and nutrition.

There are no classes in most veterinary schools on structure. There are anatomy classes, which include horses and cows, chickens and pigs, dogs and cats, reptiles and birds—inside and out. However, anatomy and structure can be two very different things. Most veterinary schools provide no classes on movement. Remember, the title is "School of Veterinary Medicine." Vets are medical professionals, not dog professionals, and there are major empirical distinctions between a "veterinarian" and a "dog person." And both are required for the well-being of show dogs.

What veterinarians are not taught, however, is not the problem. The problem is getting a veterinarian to admit that his or her knowledge of dogs may be limited to pathology, diagnosis and treatment. The challenge is to find a veterinarian who is open to your knowledge and concerns as a dog person. If you find such a vet, you have found a valuable partner. Take good care of this partner. Pay your bills on time. Remember your vet during the holiday season. A good vet is a real find.

2. The second step is to put each dog on a grooming table every week. In order to know what condition your dogs are in, you must regularly have your hands on them. You need to check their coats, their weight, their skin, their mouths, their ears, their feet, etc, on a regular basis if you want to keep them in show condition. The key is to catch and resolve a physical problem before it impairs the dog's well-being and show career.

Watering and Elimination

Two of the most important points in maintaining a dog's general health while traveling and showing are to ensure the dog is drinking enough water and eliminating regularly.

First, a little lemon juice in the dogs' water is an easy-to-use diuretic. Then, provide the dogs ample opportunities to relieve themselves.

Learn to use ex-pens for the right reasons. The most common cause of sick dogs at dog shows is that they do not drink enough water and they do not urinate enough. When you put a dog in an ex-pen, give it the opportunity to relieve itself numerous times and to take a drink a dozen times, if it wants.

Dogs at shows should be given a minimum of an hour twice a day in ex-pens. Walks are for relieving boredom and for exercising, but a dog has access to drinking water only before or after a walk. Ex-pens are for drinking, eliminating and stretching legs—maybe even changing the scenery—but drinking and eliminating are the necessities to meet.

When you're on the road, stick to bottled water if the tap water has an odor. Use it both in watering the dogs and in preparing their food.

If you live in or are traveling to a region inclined toward freezing weather in the winter and you have any outside water buckets, coat the inside of each bucket with margarine or Pam. This will keep the ice from sticking to the bucket, which makes it easier to remove the surface slab of ice each morning. Providing water is useless if the dog is unable to drink it.

In order to help a dog eliminate solid waste regularly when on a show circuit, try "matching" the dog. This involves wetting the sulfur heads of two or three paper matches, then inserting the matches (sulfur end first) into the anus. This is usually just enough of an irritant to stimulate the dog to eliminate in order to expel the matches. The sulfur is nontoxic and almost always works. If matching fails, however, the next thing to try is suppositories for infants. Dogs must eliminate regularly in order to stay healthy, and it's our responsibility to see that they do.

Matching is also the easiest way to teach dogs to use exercise pens. When ex-pen training, remember that you want to make the dog enjoy show experiences. We dog people sometimes go about teaching in a backwards manner, and ex-pen training is a good example. Typically, we put dogs in an ex-pen, and we wait and wait and wait. Once the dogs eliminate, we reward them by sticking them back in crates. This approach gives dogs little or no reason to eliminate quickly.

In ex-pen training, "match" the dog before putting him or her in the pen; the dog eliminates quickly, you give lots of praise and then the dog gets to stay in the pen as a reward for using it properly.

The same approach should apply to walks. Match the dogs before the walk, praise them for eliminating and then take them for a good long walk as a reward. Eventually, your dogs will eliminate as soon as possible so they can go for a walk.

We have also matched dogs before air travel; this can eliminate almost all accidents en route.

Hot-Weather Protection

Many breeds have a difficult time with hot weather. One of the worst things is to keep such a dog in an air-conditioned vehicle at a show, then take it out to perform in an outdoor ring in hot weather. It isn't great for you either, but it's much worse for the dog.

To minimize the problem, use a fiberglass crate with a metal-grate floor specifically made for that crate. Fill the floor beneath the metal grate with frozen chemical ice packs. Replace the metal grate so the dogs can't get to the ice packs and then put a blanket or a dog rug on top of the metal grate (because the metal can freeze). Then leave the crate outside in the heat.

The temperature inside the crate can be maintained as much as 20 degrees cooler than the outside temperature; however, the dogs are breathing the air in which they will be running and performing. This helps them avoid the shock of extreme temperature changes before they show. The majority of dogs that die at shows die because of the heat, and there is absolutely no excuse for it.

One of the most useful inventions I have seen to combat the effects of hot weather is the battery-powered crate fan. I would use crate fans to protect any heat-sensitive dog in high-temperature situations. These fans are invaluable for road trips, as you can purchase an adapter that plugs into a cigarette lighter, so it can provide airflow throughout long days on the road and still be operational for any emergency. Moreover, a crate fan on the front of a crate can be a tremendous help for dogs that get carsick.

Figure 5-01: Crate fan

During summer show season, it is helpful to keep a powdered electrolyte supplement on hand. Adding a little to their food will help keep their electrolytes in balance, which will help them handle the stress of hot show trips. The least expensive way to go is to buy the electrolyte solution for poultry—it is sold in most feed stores. For a 50-pound dog, a quarter to a half of a teaspoon added to each meal (I feed my dogs twice a day) is sufficient.

You can use Pediolyte (available at any grocery store or drugstore), but it's much more expensive. Pediolyte is best used when a dog has diarrhea, runs a fever, or is on antibiotics. Add it to their water—a half-and-half mixture—or use it straight. Dogs will be more likely to drink the mixture if you get the unflavored Pediolyte. It works to rebalance their electrolytes, which gets their systems back to normal much quicker.

Crates and Air Travel

Our favorite crates for home are furniture crates. Any cabinetmaker can build them to match the rest of your furniture, and they can be used as end tables. The insides are varathaned or finished with Formica for easy cleaning and to resist odor absorbency.

Situate the crates, then have a party at your house and see if anyone notices you have dogs in all of your tables (as long as the dogs are quiet). Also, should you be the only dog person in your home, furniture crates can keep peace with the rest of the family, since they disguise the fact that you have dog crates all over the house. (One crate maker told us his best-selling items were crates that doubled as nightstands in bedrooms. Most of us have little space in our bedrooms to add crates, so just make the furniture multipurpose.)

When you're on the road, the best crates we have found to use are the airline-approved fiberglass crates. It can be scary to take a road trip with dogs in wire crates, due to the fact that the impact of a car accident can break the wires at the welds. At worst, broken wires can impale the dog if they bend inward. At best, the damaged crate can make removing the dog safely very problematic. If you wish to use wire crates for road travel, the safest are crates designed with the smallest space between wires, such as Kennel Aire. These types of wire crates have the least potential for disaster.

When traveling by air, especially during the summer months, avoid transporting dogs in aluminum crates. Heat is the dangerous element here. If you can't touch the outside of a crate on the tarmac of an airport, imagine what the heat buildup is like inside the crate. (This is the only type of crate we have ever seen a seasoned show dog panic in, so our assumption was an intolerable buildup of heat.)

As I mentioned earlier, one of the most exciting products to come on the market is the battery-operated crate fan. It is capable of moving an enormous amount of air and attaches securely to the outside of the crate door. Personally, I would never fly another dog without one of these fans on the crate.

The average exhibitor is destined to fly with dogs to at least three shows–Westminister, the National Specialty and the AKC/Eukanuba National Championship (and it is wise for all exhibitors to make these shows as often as possible). For airline travel, the only thing you need to put in the dog's crate before a flight is paper towels. It takes three rolls to fill a 400-size crate.

This is a good job for your kids or your neighbor's kids, because each sheet needs to be torn off the roll and thrown in the crate one at a time. Just toss the sheets in and let them fall as they may. The trick then is convincing the dogs to go in the crates, because they won't think there's any room left for them.

As soon as they go in, nose around and circle a couple of times, they find it quite comfortable. Paper towels are excellent insulation against both heat and cold. Moreover, when you fly a dog, there is always the chance that the dog may have an accident. A normal, clean-living house dog that has an accident in its crate will usually spend the rest of the trip trying to bury it. They can bury their "accidents" in paper towels without any damage to the leather on their noses or to any other part of their bodies. Also, they rarely get any of the "accident" on themselves, due to the absorbency of the paper towels. (This is also a great approach when transporting puppies by air.)

In your carry-on baggage, pack a plastic garbage bag and the dog's regular bedding. When you land, if the dog has made a mess, put the paper towels in the garbage bag, which you deposit in the nearest trash receptacle at the airport. Replace the paper towels with the bedding for the trip to the hotel or home.

Before you fly with your dog, contact the American Dog Owners Association (ADOA) for the most current information about travel crates (see Resources section of this book). Priscilla Benkin does an enormous amount of research to help keep our dogs safe in air travel, and the ADOA publishes her reports.

Be aware that the airlines are tightening their cargo regulations. To find out what the most current regulations are, you can call (301) 734-7833.

They will send you a copy of the current rules. Air travel is becoming more problematic because of the inconsistencies in how regulations are interpreted. One woman flying to the Doberman National was prohibited from flying her dog in even a 700-size crate because the airline personnel would not allow the dog to fly in a crate in which even the dog's ears touched the crate ceiling.

The most current air travel regulations state that a dog must be able to stand up and turn around comfortably in its crate. What the airlines seem to be unaware of is the risk posed by a spacious crate when a dog is flying. Too much space means the dogs may fall during take-offs or landings and injure themselves.

We want our dogs to be most comfortable lying down—the safest position they can be in during a flight. Be that as it may, the main point is to be prepared for different interpretations when you enter the airport. Flexibility and adaptability will keep your blood pressure down and keep the airlines amiable toward all of us who fly with our dogs.

Before shipping a dog, check the AKC website (www.akc.org) for the most current shipping regulations, which AKC does try to keep current.

Collars and Leads

There is a sound reason for everything that a good handler does. Take the issue of leads and collars.

It doesn't matter what you show dogs on after they understand what you ask and expect of them. However, the easiest way to teach show dogs what you want and expect, without being set up to make mistakes, is to teach them on a choke collar.

All collars cause coat damage, but the collar that causes the most damage is the Obedience-type chain with rings linked together. Every time you pull on this kind of choke chain, any hair that gets caught between the rings will break or be cut. Collars known as snake, jeweled, or hexagon chains will do the least amount of coat damage. (There is also a choke collar called The Coat Saver, which is often in use in the German Shepherd ring but is good with many other coat types as well.)

Teaching with the use of a nylon choke collar is preferable; however, do not use a thin nylon collar for teaching, as it can be quite uncomfortable for the dog. Most importantly, use a choke collar for teaching *only after* you know how to position and use it correctly:

1. Put the collar on as an Obedience collar. That means the ring attached to the lead is over the back of the neck, with the lead on the right-hand side of the dog.

Figure 5-02: Chokes (top to bottom) — Coat Saver, Obedience, snake and nylon

Figure 5-03: Adjusting collar position

Figure 5-04: Setting collar position

2. With the collar rings and lead held in your left hand between the dog's ears, use the index finger of your right hand to pull the collar forward under the chin as far as it will go. While you are still holding on lightly under the chin, pull the collar up and back with your left hand. This will position the collar around the bone structure of the head almost in the same fashion as you would pick up a puppy in a suspended position (see Chapter 2, p 31).

3. Once you have the collar correctly positioned, the dog will accept your control and understand you are the boss, because the dog has

only restricted use of its neck muscles and you have control of its head.
From this point on, just repositioning the collar will remind the dog that you
are in charge. While you are teaching the dog this concept, immediately
reward the dog when it responds in accordance with your expectation.

Figure 5-05: Rolled-leather collar and tube collar

Figure 5-06: Show lead, blade snap and bolt snap

Although a nylon choke collar is more damaging to the dog's coat
(nylon causes static and static breaks hair), it is still my choice for teaching,
because it is much easier to keep in position. Once the lesson is over, however, remove the collar. It is advisable to avoid using any kind of nylon collar as a show dog's daily collar, since it will do enormous damage to the coat.
The one exception is a "tube collar." This kind of collar has no edges that
can cut hair, and all of the seams are on the outside, away from the coat. A
tube collar can be made from a variety of materials, one of which is nylon.
The other type of collar that does the least amount of coat damage and is
therefore a good choice to leave on is a rolled-leather collar.

When you are teaching, I recommend using only leather leads. Any
other kind of lead can burn or cut your hand if it scrapes across your skin,
and you're more likely to let go of the lead should that happen. Leather is
the safest, most reliable lead to use for teaching purposes.

If you're going to use a leather lead with a snap on it, use a blade snap
to ensure you're not going to lose your dog in the process of its education.
A bolt-type snap can and does open accidentally.

Our favorite show leads had no snaps on them. They are permanently attached to the collar and they have a swivel, so the lead remains untangled without any work on your part.

Bait

If you are going to bait a dog, the bait to use is liver (or another type of organ meat). Buy frozen-sliced liver (in the grocer's freezer section or on a meat tray—not in a cup—in the meat department), so each piece is the same thickness all the way through.

1. Put the liver—either frozen or thawed—in a pan of water heavily seasoned with garlic salt. Boil the liver on the stove while you preheat your oven to 350 degrees Fahrenheit.

2. Once you've cooked it long enough for the garlic salt to penetrate, take it off the stove and rinse the liver in cold-running water, thoroughly cleaning it to remove any residue from the boiling. Set three or four layers of paper towels on a cookie sheet, and put the liver on the paper towels.

3. Turn your preheated oven to "Off," and then put the cookie sheet in the oven so the liver can dry. It takes the same amount of time to dry the outside of the liver (while keeping the inside moist and flavorful) as it does to cool your oven. The garlic salt helps to preserve the liver, thus preventing sliminess and stomach upsets. Warning: Never put paper in a stove that is "On."

If you're going someplace where you may not have access to refrigeration or a cooler, freeze the cooked liver in baggies (a couple of slices per bag) while it is still warm. Before you start out on your trip, take the baggie containing the frozen liver out of the freezer and fill it with rock salt. As the liver thaws, it will absorb the salt, which in turn helps to preserve it. This will keep the liver good for about one week. Before you use the liver, however, remember to wash it thoroughly, as it would be extremely salty otherwise.

The reasons to use liver are:

❖ Almost all dogs like it.
❖ It is one of the least messy baits to use.
❖ The garlic salt encourages dogs to drink more water, which makes them urinate more, which keeps them healthier on the road.
❖ Liver is one of the highest sources of energy.

Honing the Show Attitude

The next concept is difficult to grasp and even more difficult to practice, but it can pay off. It is one of the major advantages that professional handlers have over owner-handlers. No matter how spoiled your dogs are at home (and I am a firm believer that dogs should be spoiled–but not spoiled bratty), when you get in your vehicle to go to a show, learn to ignore your dogs. What you want to teach them is that they will get your undivided attention only in the ring.

If your dogs get to run and play in the park, go to McDonald's for lunch, and sleep on the bed, why in heaven's name would they want to go to a dog show? But if they're sleeping in crates and being properly taken care of, but not pampered or catered to until show time, then the dogs will usually be willing to give you 110 percent, because they learn to look forward to all of the attention that you are going to give them at that time. (A dog should spend only as much time in a crate as it normally spends sleeping. Other hours should be spent exercising, feeding and working with the dog.)

You will be astonished at what a difference this kind of approach can make in the show attitude of a dog. And dogs adapt very quickly. When dogs of one breed are traveling with a handler, they even learn which dogs they follow as each is taken out for showing. You can see their excitement: "Oh boy, I'm next!" It is one of the reasons dogs with professional handlers usually show better than dogs with their owner-handlers.

MISCELLANEOUS TIPS

The following are random morsels of wisdom we have gathered along our way. I offer them here as food for thought:

❖ **If you're a breeder and you always name litters with easily recognizable theme names, it gains you years of peer recognition.** The more people encounter your kennel name and your theme names, the quicker they will know who you are and what you breed. This is a great help to breeders, especially to novice breeders.

❖ **When you have a bitch that is due to whelp, add a little bit of baking soda to all water she has access to a day or so before whelping.** It helps to neutralize acid milk, thus helping to reduce the chance of colicky puppies.

❖ **If you have neonates on the ground, consider adding a litter box with litter material made from paper (such as Purina's Second Nature) to the pen when the puppies are between 3 and 4 weeks old.** The litter material is harmless to puppies that might chew on it, and a litter box is an excellent start to house training. If you lay a treated "piddle pad" under the litter, the puppies tend to eliminate in the litter box more readily.

Figure 5-07: Puppy in litter box
(courtesy of Mary Strom)

❖ **Try clicker-training your litters.** This approach creates some of the smartest dogs I've met and significantly decreases the risk of puppies being returned to you because of behavioral problems.

❖ **If you use exercise pens, get the cheapest ones you can find.** The more expensive pens are made of heavier-gauge wire; every time you set them up and take them down, the welding is compromised. We found that the cheapest ones were more lightweight, more flexible and more durable.

The best snaps to use to connect ex-pens are the brass snaps. They will not corrode in weather; other metals used for snaps can corrode eventually to where they will not close properly, and accidents happen.

❖ **If you use water buckets, make sure you put the bucket on a line instead of snapping it to something solid.** If the bucket is hooked to something solid and the dog gets caught, he or she can actually drown. If the bucket is hooked to a line and the dog gets caught, all it has to do is move and water will come out of the bucket.

❖ **If you are going to use ex-pens, invest in a sunscreen.** A plastic tarp over an ex-pen can increase the heat in the pen. A sunscreen allows for airflow underneath it while reducing the direct sunlight.

❖ **When it comes to pooper scoopers, buy the cheapest you can buy.** The cheaper they are, the more flexible they are and the longer they last.

❖ **You have perhaps heard that a dog can feel your tension going down the lead.** There may be some truth to that, but it is certainly true that a dog can smell adrenalin. When we are nervous, our dogs can sniff it on us. One way to help counteract this is to carry breath mints with you when you're showing, and pop a breath mint every time you walk in the ring. This is also a good idea for judges, since judges can be nervous in the ring as well, and the dogs will know it. If they sense anxiety, it can make them anxious.

❖ **When traveling in an RV, it is infinitely safer for your dogs as well as for the environment to use a capful of fabric softener in the toilet instead of toilet chemicals.** Toilet chemicals can be toxic. Also, RV toilet paper is single ply, has no perfume and is undyed. Perfumes and dyes are what make toilet paper hard to break down, so if you buy regular single-ply toilet paper without dyes or perfumes, you are getting the same quality of biodegradable paper as you would be getting with RV toilet paper but for less money.

One brief aside: When your RV is plugged in at home, regularly check the water level of the battery. A battery can use up to 50 percent more water when it is plugged in than when it's running.

❖ **To reduce the chances of disease transmission among your dogs while on the road, make a list of which dog goes in which crate and pen and stick to it.** Also, keep your pooper scoopers in disinfectant to eliminate the risk of spreading germs among your pens.

❖ **The best choice in food and water dishes for your dogs is stainless steel, glass or crockery.** Chemicals used in processing plastics can break down with age and leak into the water, which can cause the pigment on a dog's nose to fade. This effect seems to be reversible only about half the time.

❖ **Anyone with dogs also has flies.** If you plant marigolds underneath all of your windows, around your kennel and by all of your doors, flies will not come in. Flies will not fly over or around the scent of marigolds. Another option is to hang water-filled, clear-plastic, zip-lock bags (quart size) around porches or covered exercise areas. The bags must be hung in such a way as to catch direct sunlight. Flies will leave the area where these water-filled bags are hanging. Sounds amazing, and it is!

❖ **For outdoor dog beds, you can save money by making your own.** Start with No. 9 or No. 10 white-duck canvas (remnants are the cheapest way to go) and four 2x4's, 2x6's, or 2x8's (height is dependent on the weight of your dogs). Make a frame that fits whatever size piece of canvas you bought.

Nail the canvas (use only roofing nails) on the top edge of the frame. If you nail the canvas over onto the side of the frame, it will come loose the first time a dog chews on a corner of the frame.

Figure 5-08: Homemade dog bed

This kind of bed does not damage coat or hold fleas. If the canvas is not heavy duty, however, dogs will quickly find themselves unsure of their footing, so they will be less likely to use the bed. The cotton canvas will reshrink every time you hose off the bed, thus keeping it tight as a drum.

The cost for a size that can accommodate an adult Doberman is approximately $10 to $20, and the bed will last for years. These are great beds to use in doghouses, because it will keep the dog off the ground.

❖ **Cedar chips or shavings are unadvisable in some circumstances.** Cedar stains when it gets wet, which can spell disaster for white dogs. Also, puppies can get quite ill if they eat cedar. So for puppies or white dogs, choose another type of bedding material.

❖ **Skunk odor is an age-old problem for people with dogs.** One option for eliminating this odor on your dog is to wash the dog down with liquid fabric softener. Tomato juice works, but oh, the mess! Have you ever poured tomato juice on a dog whose first inclination is to shake when dowsed with any kind of liquid? Suddenly, you have an art deco washroom. And vinegar works well, but oh, the smell–for days.

The least disruptive option we have found is to kill the odor with straight fabric softener, give the dog a regular bath, and then spray it down with diluted fabric softener.

Another option, if you happen to have the supplies, is to bathe the dog with a solution made up of 1 quart of hydrogen peroxide (3 percent), 1/4 cup of baking soda and 1 teaspoon of liquid dish soap. Mix in a bucket, and then saturate the dog's coat with the solution, using a sponge. Once the coat is saturated and has set for 10-15 minutes, bathe the dog. If you use this option, do not store the mixture; it can become volatile in a closed container (sort of a dog fancier's Molotov cocktail).

❖ **The best group of products I have found to eliminate a variety of doggie odors is Nature's Odor & Germ Control (aka Non Scents).** The single ingredient is a type of rock that absorbs odors naturally and is non-toxic. Three of my favorite products are the Household Packs, the Carpet Granules and the Pet Powder.

The Household Pack is excellent in whelping rooms and cars. When the packs stop working, you just lay them in direct sunlight for a day or so. After that, the packs are like new. The Carpet Granules are excellent for absorbing doggie odor in carpets. Just sprinkle onto the carpet and leave for a day or two. Then vacuum up the granules. The Pet Powder is excellent after expressing anal glands and to neutralize the odor given off by a bitch in season. At my seminars, we often used the Pet Powder on all of the bitches in season and not once did any of the male dogs take note of them! The powder is completely safe to apply directly on dogs.

❖ **It can be risky to use any pine products in your housecleaning, if you have dogs.** Most pine products are made with concentrated pine oil, which can be toxic to a dog's liver. Even scrubbing the kitchen floor with a pine product can be dangerous; the dog walks across the floor and later licks its feet.

This routine can cause a buildup of the pine oil, and you run the risk of the dog developing liver problems later in life. You needn't worry about pine cones, pine shavings, or pine boughs, since they do not contain concentrated oils.

❖ **Carpet fresheners have been known to cause toxic reactions in dogs, so avoid using them if you have carpeting in your house.**

❖ **When preparing to have new wall-to-wall carpet laid in your home, talk to your installer about laying Visquene between the pad and the carpet.** It makes the carpet much easier to keep clean and prevents odors from working down into the pad.

❖ **If you are staying in hotels or motels, first thing to do is to close the toilet lid.** Public accommodations may use chemicals in the toilet that can kill dogs.

❖ **One of the easiest ways to improve coat condition is to use a humidifier in whatever room your dogs spend the most time, be it a bedroom, the kitchen or a kennel.** Even in humid areas, most homes and kennels are heated and air-conditioned, which generally removes a considerable amount of humidity from the air. Dry air dries out hair and generates static electricity.

❖ **If you have show dogs, it's a good idea to have an aloe vera plant in your house.** The natural enzymes of the plant's slimy insides work incredibly well to heal cut pads. Even a pad that is cut severely enough to where your vet recommends wrapping it and keeping the dog off of the foot can be healed in a matter of a few days if you use aloe vera. But it must be directly from the plant. There are many aloe vera products on the market, most of which are totally ineffectual, because processing destroys the enzymes that speed healing.

In our experience, aloe vera is only miraculous in healing cut pads, although it can be helpful in other situations.

❖ **Aspirin, applied to the skin, can work wonders on lick sores. For lick sores, or lick granulomas, apply a greasy substance, such as Vaseline or Neosporin ointment.** Crush an aspirin and sprinkle the power on the greased surface. Then wrap the area with VetWrap, and leave it for three days. The wound will fill in, and the dog will leave it alone.

❖ **For lickers and chewers, try oil of cloves.** It naturally anesthetizes the irritated area and tastes horrid, so it strongly discourages dogs to continue licking or chewing.

❖ **Chewing can sometimes be caused by a mineral deficiency.** Try giving your dog a kelp supplement for 10 days only.

❖ **One of the best all-around healing agents I have found is Chris Christensen's Peace & Kindness.** This product contains colloidal silver, which is anti-viral, anti-bacterial and anti-fungal. Peace & Kindness seems to heal just about anything–from hot spots and burns to cuts and scrapes. It can even be effective against rashes.

❖ **The Bite Not collar is a considerable improvement over the Elizabethan collar.** It is similar to a human neck brace and includes ties to keep it secure even on dogs with heads of similar or smaller width than their necks. To learn more, call 1-800-424-8366 or go to www.bitenot.com .

❖ **If you have a bitch that's due to come in season, you can save your male dogs unnecessary stimulation by giving the bitch chlorophyll tablets just before and during her heat.** Human brands are usually much less expensive than brands for dogs. A 50-pound dog would get two pills twice a day. Chlorophyll tablets prevent the odor from permeating the air. A male allowed to smell her or her urine will know, but you won't have males coming from miles around to park themselves on your doorstep for three weeks.

If you're going to breed her, take her off of the pills a couple of days before the breeding. After all, you wouldn't want to teach a stud dog to associate the smell of chlorophyll with a bitch in season.

Another option is to apply Nature's Odor & Germ Control Pet Powder on and around your bitch's vulva frequently; it must be reapplied each time she urinates.

❖ **If you have a male dog that is ultrasensitive to bitches in season or has an excessive interest in sniffing the ground, randomly put vanilla extract on his nose and whiskers (if he has whiskers).** A dog usually cannot smell through the odor of vanilla. It has to be done randomly at home, so he just thinks you're a little whacky and this is just one of the odd (but innocuous) things you do to him.

Keep the vanilla in your tack box so that every time you go to a dog show, vanilla on the nose is simply part of the normal grooming procedure you go through for a show; that way, the dog's concentration will be undisturbed by any bitches in season at the show. Vanilla is long lasting and non-irritating. Other products, such as menthol or Vicks, can irritate them and are short lived.

Common sense is the key to all you do. If you are doing advanced Obedience with your dog, common sense tells us the dog is going to need his olfactory prowess for such an activity. Therefore, the use of vanilla is ridiculous in this case.

❖ **Many dogs, particularly males, develop a urine odor that seems to hang around the dog whether it's urinating or not.** First, check to make sure there is no medical reason for this. If the dog is healthy, the acid content in their system may be a possible cause. Altering the acid content of their system—higher or lower—will, in most cases, eliminate the odor. The easiest thing to try is Vitamin C; you can try vinegar, but Vitamin C is easier. An antacid works well on toy dogs, but large breeds would require incredibly large doses.

❖ **Changing the acid content of a dog's system can reduce the amount of coat staining from saliva, tears or urine.** One option is to add apple cider vinegar to a dog's water supply.

❖ **If you must induce vomiting, use hydrogen peroxide.** You can give your dog 1 to 3 teaspoons of hydrogen peroxide every 10 minutes until vomiting occurs, but no more than three times. If the dog does not vomit after the third application, get the dog to your vet.

❖ **For common intestinal irregularities, add a large spoonful of canned pumpkin (unseasoned) to the dog's food.** This can help the dog through diarrhea or constipation, and pumpkin is a usable nutrient. For an older dog, sprinkling Metamucil over the food can help regulate his or her bowels (note that Metamucil may cause gas in some dogs).

❖ **Coconut macaroons can help to eliminate stress-induced diarrhea.**

❖ **Another approach to doggie diarrhea is Imodium.** Give 1 mg per 15 pounds of body weight, 1 or 2 times per day.

❖ **Charcoal tablets for people (available in most drug stores) are very useful for dogs with gas.** The only drawback is that charcoal absorbs not only gas but any oral medications the dog might be on. So avoid using charcoal if your dogs are on oral medication.

❖ **If your dogs enjoy chewing on wood, an easy thing to try is to spread a paste of water and alum (used to put the pucker in pickles) on any wood the dogs gnaw on outside.** The paste is messy, so it's best for outdoor use only. Once the dog tastes the alum, he or she will generally stop chewing wood altogether.

It is imperative that you do everything you can to prevent your dogs from chewing on pressure-treated wood (used for fencing and decking). Most such wood is treated with arsenic, which can have a horrible effect on dogs.

❖ **Yeast and fungi thrive in a damp environment.** Athlete's foot powder can help prevent the growth of yeast and other organisms that cause infections in dogs' ears or on dogs' feet. It is especially helpful to dogs that swim frequently or dogs with allergies.

❖ **For dogs that are fearful of thunderstorms or fireworks, try a dab of oil of peppermint on each of the dog's pads.** This may have a calming effect. If it doesn't help, you've not wasted your money, because ants will evacuate an area treated with oil of peppermint; mice aren't real keen about it either.

❖ **If you have dog houses or dog beds in your kennel runs, make sure the houses or beds are situated near the gate.** Dogs have a tendency to eliminate as far away from where they sleep as possible. With the house or bed near the gate, eliminations will be at the other end of the run.

This idea comes under the heading of making your work as easy as possible. Who needs feces right in front of the run entrance, where it is easily smeared by opening the gate and where the dogs would run through it to jump on you in a glorious, albeit odoriferous and messy, greeting?

❖ **If you have dogs that make "mud wallow lines" in the yard during the winter or rainy season, lay down hay (not straw).** This will help keep the dogs cleaner and will re-seed the area. Come spring when you pick up the hay, you should have a nice new layer of tough cover.

❖ **The rubbery shelf liner (available in most grocery and hardware stores) also makes an excellent hair remover.** Keep a piece in your car for fast hair removal from clothes. It also works wonders when laid under the metal tray of a wire crate, virtually eliminating all noise.

❖ **For odor buildup outdoors, try this amazing recipe: Mix 1 quart of water, 1 cup of lemon-scented dish soap, 1 cup of lemon-scented ammonia, 1 capful of mint-flavored mouthwash.** Pour this mixture into a garden sprayer and spray away. It's very sudsy, but don't rinse. The mixture is totally safe to dogs and other species; however, it does kill bugs. It lasts a long time; I usually do just two or three applications a year.

❖ **The pads of a dog's feet harden in the fall. Soften them by rubbing in oil or cream.** This increases grip and traction for indoor shows, particularly if the rings are carpeted (such as at Westminster or the AKC/Eukanuba National Championship).

❖ **It is inadvisable to let dogs chew on anything hard enough to drive a nail with.** Hooves, for instance, can be dangerous to the integrity of a dog's teeth.

❖ **If you live with dogs that tend toward fighting, keep a canned air horn handy.** These horns are available at any marine supply store and work instantly to break up most fights. Even if it distracts them momentarily, that's enough time to separate them.

❖ **If you have dogs that eat at the speed of light, slow them down.** One sure way to do this is to add a billiard ball to their food dish. It's usually too heavy and too slick for dogs to pick up so they have to keep moving it around in order to get to the food.

❖ **Never give a dog Ibuprofen.** It damages the liver. For infrequent swelling or stiffness, a children's aspirin is usually sufficient.

TIPS FOR THE DOG-SHOW NOVICE

Remember, all of us have been where you are now—beginners or novices trying to find our way in the show world, while simultaneously trying to look like we fit in and know what we're doing. Be assured that the majority of experienced dog-show people are willing to be helpful and supportive, in return for those who were there for them when they were new to the sport. You enter the Fancy with one common bond to all others—a love of dogs.

❖ **If you are just beginning as an owner-handler, the first thing you need to know is this: The left side of the dog is always the show side.** This is the side the judge will always see in the ring.

❖ **Any owner-handler should be showing at Canadian Kennel Club (CKC), United Kennel Club (UKC), States Kennel Club (SKC) or International shows or whatever else might be available to you in your area.** You only gain confidence by winning. All of these shows are more informal, more relaxed and slower-paced than AKC shows. Also, professional handlers are less likely to be in force at these events, so your chances of winning more frequently are better. If you can go to these shows, you'll have a more comfortable environment in which to learn not only how to show your dog but also how to win, and that will increase your chances of winning when you come back to the AKC shows.

❖ **Read all you can—learn all you can.** The more information you have, the more you will use your own discrimination about how best to care for your dogs, how best to go about planning your breeding program. The more your read, study and learn, the more variety of opinions and information you will take in. And just like our dogs can be taught to learn, we can learn to think. There is a bibliography at the end of this book to get you started.

❖ **Become so familiar with your show lead that you no longer think about it.** Pick a place in your house where you frequently sit, be it your favorite television chair or telephone chair. Fasten the show lead to the left front leg of that chair. Every time you sit there, pick up the lead and practice folding it in and out of your hand, until you stop thinking about how to do it.

Next, fasten some keys to your show lead, and practice running with the lead, reeling it in and out, until you do it without rattling the keys. This exercise will teach you balance and smoothness of motion.

❖ **Do not enter in the Novice Class.** When you're a novice, you need to be in one of the larger classes. This allows you more time to watch and learn from experienced exhibitors. The Novice Class is usually small and offers little in the way of experience to study.

❖ **One of the fastest ways to increase your knowledge about movement is to go to the Doberman ring and watch.** Almost always the breed has a decent entry; the dogs are tall enough to where you can really watch the legs; there is no coat, color or pattern issues to cause optical illusions when they move; it is a breed shown hands off, for the most part; and the quality of Dobermans is usually quite good. For these reasons, you might learn a lot by watching Dobermans move in the ring.

❖ **In order to spend money wisely when showing dogs, it's important to learn how to group your shows.** Sit down and figure out how many shows you can afford to enter in a year. If you can afford to go to 12 shows a year, and you go to one per month, you may never finish your dog, because every time you walk into the show ring, it's a new experience for you and for the dog, and you're both nervous and don't quite know what's going on.

If you can go to 12 shows per year and decide to do a three-day weekend four times a year, it can make a major difference in your ability to win. The first day, you get the nervousness out of the way; the second day, you're getting it together; by the third day, the odds are in your favor. By grouping your shows, then, you increase your chances of winning.

❖ **If you are willing do the kind of work that a professional handler does to prepare for a show, you as an owner-handler have the edge over professional handlers the majority of the time.** Good judges are always on the lookout for new dogs. And when you only have one dog, while a handler may have 10 to 20 dogs to keep track of, you have a significant advantage—time and focus. Make the most of this advantage in your grooming, choice of clothing, support, etc.

❖ **I am a firm believer in stewarding at shows.** Being a ring steward, you can learn that much more about the workings of the show ring; it gives you an opportunity to pay back a bit of what shows have given you; and if there are two dogs in the ring of equal quality, the judge just might point to the dog handled by someone familiar. That's not politics; that's human nature. Stewarding is also a great way to network.

❖ **Show and breed not what can be finished but what should be finished.**

One last thought along the lines of dog wherewithal: I am firm in my belief that dogs should be allowed to be dogs. All of us have dogs because we love dogs. An artificial or sterile life is not much of a life—not for a person or a dog. Let them be what they were born to be.

Enter the gene pool at your own risk. There is no lifeguard on duty.
—Susan Lybrand

canine structure in the show ring

When evaluating your dog for show, remember that evaluating adult dogs is entirely different than evaluating puppies. With puppies, you look for anything that could be a structural challenge or problem to help ensure the puppy is placed in the best kind of home or lifestyle for that puppy's physical capabilities. With an adult dog, you always want to look at its virtues first.

A valuable habit to form is to find and verbalize five desirable qualities in any dog before you say one bad thing about it. Then when you look at the faults, you will be more likely to put them in perspective—weigh them against the qualities you verbalized. Do the qualities outweigh the faults?

Try this at ringside, even with your most formidable competitor's dog. Never say anything bad about a dog, not even to yourself, until you have said five good things about it. Not only will it make you a better dog person, but you may find the approach to be contagious.

Be warned: One of the worst faults is to imagine your dog has no faults. Like all other living things, no dog is perfect. Convincing yourself that your dog is perfect is one of the worst mistakes you can make. After all, you can make no improvements if you are unwilling to see or unable to understand what needs to be improved. Deluding yourself into thinking your dog is flawless could diminish your credibility in the dog world.

Do everything in your power to learn all you can about both canine structure and breed standards. All too often, people tend to learn only what is within their immediate interest, so their knowledge remains limited. You can't blame people for not knowing what they don't know. However, greater respect is earned by those who live their lives as students. To the best of your ability, always broaden your horizons beyond your immediate boundaries.

STRUCTURAL REVIEW

Some of the most significant words of wisdom I was fortunate enough to receive over the years were: A sound dog will age more gracefully, be less likely to break down from stress or injury, experience less fatigue and greater efficiency in work, and stay healthier and more attractive throughout its life.

It has been suggested that correct structure is less significant in the conformation ring than the *illusion* of correctness. I take great exception to this view, because accepting the illusion of correctness is simply a quick route to undoing the overall quality of a breed.

For instance, take a dog that is clean coming and going. One might assume soundness in this picture, but what if this clean movement is actually the result of the dog being straight in both the front and rear assemblies? Straightness can cause tighter joints, which in turn gives the *illusion* of clean motion.

Both the Chinese Shar-Pei and the Bulldog standards call for their respective breeds to be higher in the rear than at the withers. A judge must be able to consider whether that requirement is met as the result of a virtue or a fault. Suppose the high rear is caused by slipped hocks, which many times encourages the dog to stiffen or lock the joint in place in order to prevent it from falling or collapsing forward and thus raises the height of the rear assembly. In such a case, the high rear is caused by a fault instead of a virtue.

To judge a dog strictly on the illusion of correctness invariably results in rewarding some dogs for the faults that create the illusion. We must distinguish between sound structure and the illusion of sound structure and, for the sake of our breeds' futures, strive for true soundness.

Sound structure is as imperative for Obedience and working dogs as it is for show dogs—sometimes, even more so. For example, the more you exercise a dog with wide shoulders, the worse those shoulders will become.

If a dog's shoulders are not formed properly around the ribcage, they tend to muscle under the blade. If the shoulders fit tight, the muscles form over the shoulder.

Another example is in the whole of a dog's front assembly. If the front assembly is unsound, the dog could break down from repetitive jumping. And it isn't the amount of jumping done in the Obedience or Agility ring that wears the structure out; it is the hundreds of practice jumps the dog does getting ready for competition.

Sixty to seventy-five percent of a dog's weight is carried in the front half of its body. When dogs jump, they push off with their rear legs and land on their front legs. Therefore, every time a dog lands on an unsound front assembly, the tissues give and stretch until finally they wear out.

A well-trained dog will go beyond its physical limitations to do what we ask until it has nothing left to give, and it is grossly unfair of us to ask more of a dog than it is physically structured to give.

And what happens when dogs reach the point of breakdown? The average owner's initial tendency is to get frustrated with the dog. More times than I can count, my husband and I were approached by someone wanting to know why their dog suddenly wouldn't take the jumps after so many good performances in the Obedience ring. These people wanted to know why their dogs were suddenly being disobedient or just plain lazy.

In almost every case we encountered, the dog's structure had broken down. Most people are genuinely unaware of their dogs' physical condition when such behavior patterns begin to emerge. The body is simply telling the dog it cannot do another jump. How long before the dog reaches this point of breakdown depends largely on the owner's awareness of and respect for the dog's inherent physical strengths and weaknesses.

A dog or bitch with seriously unsound structure needs to be spayed or neutered and placed in a home that will ask of it only what it can handle. Some poorly structured dogs are best suited to homes where they can be free to be couch potatoes. Some just need homes where the most that is expected of them is to run and play with the kids. However, a dog with structural issues still needs to be kept in good physical condition. No dog should be allowed to get fat, but excess weight is particularly hard on a dog with structural issues. It is very important to keep all dogs in good physical condition, as the better a dog's muscling is, the better it can cope with stresses on its structure. This also aids in greater blood flow to bones and joints. A dog with structural issues may be unsuitable as a working or performance dog, but they can still be good company on an evening stroll or romping freely in the backyard.

Inherent Structural Challenges

Slipped hocks are a very common structural fault that can physically impair a dog. Despite such structural weaknesses, dogs will do Obedience work and Herding, Lure Coursing and Agility, until they are no longer able to physically meet these challenges. Is that fair to do this to the dogs we profess to love? But when placed in a pet home, a dog with slipped hocks will probably have few difficulties.

With slipped hocks, sporting dogs can become worthless in the field because there is no stability on rough ground. Swimming dogs may take a dislike to water, because a dog needs stability in its rear legs in order to swim well. If the hock is flopping around, the dog probably will high-tail it out of the water and tell you to go get the duck yourself. Herding dogs and coursing dogs generally lose the ability to make fast corners safely. Earth dogs lose the ability to go into or back out of a lair. A Toy dog with slipped hocks can end up with an altered temperament due to pain.

Figure 6-01: Golden Retriever with slipped hocks (courtesy of Shereen Farber)

Once the tissue in a joint wears out, chances are it will develop arthritis as the dog ages.

Luxating patellas (knees) are a very different problem from slipped hocks. Slipped hocks are caused by a tissue problem. Slipped or luxating patellas can be caused by either a tissue or bone problem, but they can be surgically repaired, whereas to date no procedure has been developed to repair slipped hocks.

It is best to have your vet check the dog's knees instead of checking them yourself, because it's very easy to hurt the dog in the process unless you know exactly what to do. However, have the knees checked only after the dog is eight weeks old, since it takes the first eight weeks for tissue to develop its natural strength. Dogs frequently seen skipping or stretching a rear leg back for no apparent reason need to have their knees checked by the vet.

Slipped or luxating patellas worked beyond their capacity or left untended can cause tremendous damage and pain. Being aware of this problem early on can save the dog a great deal of discomfort. However, bear in mind that a surgical correction makes the dog ineligible for the show ring. More importantly, luxating patellas are usually genetic, so although you may show a dog with bad knees, it would be an extremely bad idea to include that dog in a breeding program.

If you need more reasons to expand your working knowledge of canine structure, I offer these:

❖ **A dog acquired for jumping in Obedience or Agility should have no looseness in the elbows or lack in prosternum, both of which can cause stretched and damaged tissue in the front assembly.**

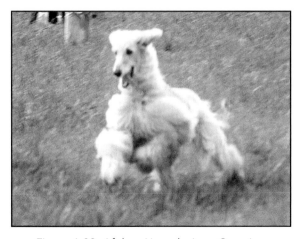

Figure 6-02: Afghan Hound—Lure Coursing

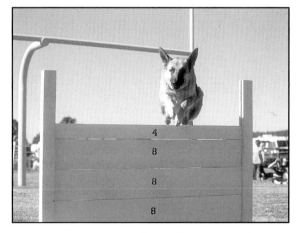

Figure 6-03: German Shepard Dog—Obedience

Figure 6-04: Chesapeake Bay Retriever—Field Trial

Figure 6-05: Siberian Huskies—Sledding

❖ **A sporting dog with a ewe neck may eventually be incapable of carrying a bird.** A water breed with a ewe neck may make a poor swimmer.

❖ **A dog bred to go to ground is fairly useless if its loin is too short or nonexistent.**

❖ **A herring gut or high hocks diminish stamina.**

❖ **An overangulated rear, which creates a form of sickle hocks, causes a poorly synchronized gait, destroying efficiency of movement.**

❖ **High shoulders are one of the most destructive weaknesses that a dog in harness can have.**

❖ **Shoulders set too close together can impede the ability of a tracking dog to keep its nose to the ground.**

❖ **Too low of a tailset interferes with an effortless gait.**

❖ **Too high of a tailset can prevent a dog from being capable of pulling a cart.**

❖ **High toes can damage the feet on a digging breed.**

We owe our dogs the effort of developing a good eye and sensitive hand to structural weaknesses. Perfection may be unattainable, but the striving yields its own rewards—and that striving must include learning all we can.

Avoidable Structural Challenges

Structure is to a great extent mandated by genetics. However, some structural problems rest squarely on our shoulders. For instance, the wrong nutrition given to puppies can result in improper structural development (see Chapter 2, p 34-35, and Chapter 3, p 62-63).

A dog's feet can be destroyed by long toenails. Tendons and ligaments do not contain the type of cells that allow for retraction if these tissues have been overextended or hyperextended. When a dog's nails touch the ground, nature provides a way out, if we do not. The foot will begin to roll in order to compensate. As the foot rolls, the tendons and ligaments begin to stretch. No dog deserves to lose the full capability of its feet, but a show dog is in part judged by what the breed standard says about the foot. Regular nail care is all it takes (see Chapter 7, p 128-129).

Figure 6-06: Short nails, sound foot

Figure 6-07: Foot damaged by long nails

Another such point involves teeth. There is no excuse for not knowing how many teeth your dog has and should have. The breeds that have a disqualification for missing teeth don't have a problem because the breeders must pay attention to counting teeth. The problem lay in the breeds that have no disqualification for or mention of missing teeth; in these breeds, the breeders don't check because they see no necessity to do so. Basics are basics, whether a breed standard addresses them or not. No standard calls for four legs, two ears or two eyes. Some things are givens, and knowing how many teeth a dog should have is one of them.

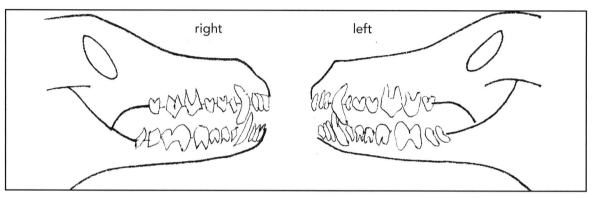

Figure 6-08: Tooth chart (courtesy of Phantom Lake Borzois)

CONDITIONING

Stay Loose

The best way to keep your dogs in condition is to teach them to be loose. Dogs that run, play, jump, twist, turn and use all speeds are going to condition their whole bodies so that they can help compensate for whatever weakness or structural faults they may have. It's the same principle as athletes cross-training; you never see athletes using just one form of exercise routine.

Just muscling the running gear doesn't compensate for anything. Playing ball and interacting with your dogs are good ways to condition them, because you can watch what they're doing and how.

If you have acreage, offer your dogs free range only at designated times. If they have access to it all the time, their enjoyment of the space will diminish (and dogs can be as lazy as we can be). However, if they live a routine life with only limited times to run loose, they will learn to run their legs off because they will perceive running time as a treat.

Large and medium-sized dogs are usually incapable of moving properly or developing to their full potential if they spend their lives exercising only in paddocks, small backyards or kennel runs. Dogs need to develop and condition the muscles that move them in straight lines. Running six or ten steps then having to turn a corner won't do it. This also applies to small dogs kept in more confined areas. People tend to scale down available space to fit the size of the dog, so small breeds sometimes end up in the same condition as large dogs that exercise in backyards.

If your dogs spend most of their time in a yard, take them out for long walks or jogs, or if possible, find an open space where they can run long, straight distances.

Road Work

Be cautious about the "virtues" of road work. I am opposed to road work as a normal routine for show dogs—so was my husband. Road work is forced exercise with the dog running alongside a mechanical device, such as a bicycle or car, or on a treadmill at a set speed for a set distance. For most dogs, road work does little or nothing to improve movement.

Road work develops the muscles needed to protect the dog's structure at a certain speed and gait. In short, road work can create generic movement in a show dog. Since different breeds and types of dogs are meant to move in different ways, however, why would we want to train them all to move the same, as if we were striving for "cookie cutter" show dogs? A Bulldog should move like a Bulldog, not like a Clumber Spaniel. A Bearded Collie should move differently from a German Shepherd. And a Miniature Pinscher would not be a "Min Pin" if it were to lose its unique motion in order to move like a Fox Terrier.

Road work can be good for building stamina and enhancing a dog's attitude. Unfortunately, most people use road work for the purpose of creating better movement in the dog; the tactic seldom works.

Cavalletti Conditioning

Most dogs fall short of their potential in reach, drive and balance due to the fact that they are not given the opportunity to develop the muscles that would enable them to use their inborn structure to its fullest. One of the ways you can help your dog achieve greater reach, drive and synchronicity of movement is through cavalletti conditioning.

The cavalletti was traditionally a series of adjustable-height timber jumps for schooling horses. With horses, the cavalletti is arranged above ground and used to teach horses to pick up their hooves and step. With dogs, however, the goal is to develop appropriate muscle groups. A canine cavalletti, then, is a series of pipes laid in an evenly spaced row on the ground (never anchored down) that the dog must gait across.

A canine cavalletti should consist of between 7 and 10 pieces of PCV pipe; the number of pipes is dependent on the size of the area you have available for the conditioning sessions. I prefer white PCV pipe, as it is most visible to the dog. The length of the pipes is dependent on the size of the dog. For a large dog, 3-foot lengths are usually sufficient. You want enough width that your dog isn't tempted to jump off of the course while working.

Figure 6-09: Cavalletti layout
(courtesy of Mary Strom)

The diameter of the pipes is dependant on the surface on which they are to be laid. A 1-inch diameter is fine for a very flat surface, but it probably would not show in grass or be able to roll in gravel.

You want to lay the pipes on a surface that will allow them to remain stationary on their own, such as grass, gravel, dirt or carpeting. Surfaces such as hardwood floors, linoleum or cement will not work. In order to be fair to your dog, you want the pipes to be very visible and

Figure 6-10: Dog going over cavallettis
(courtesy of Mary Strom)

stationary but instantly movable if the dog touches them.

Measure your dog from the ground to the highest point of its shoulders or withers. Lay the pipes on the ground parallel to one another, like rungs of a ladder or railroad ties. Place them the same distance apart as the height you measured on the dog. For example, if your dog measures 20 inches in height, the pipes should be spaced 20 inches apart.

Figure 6-11: Wicketing dog for spacing of cavallettis
(courtesy of Mary Strom)

Figure 6-12: Cavallettis in first placement
(courtesy of Mary Strom)

Put the dog on a collar and lead and take it to the cavalletti area. Gait the dog around the area until it is gaiting comfortably, and then gait it across the pipes. Initially, the dog may hesitate, drop its head, become distracted or lose concentration. Ignore these reactions; gait the dog around the area again and then gait it across the cavalletti again. If the dog touches a pipe with its feet, the pipe will roll; most dogs hate this, so they will start paying attention to where their feet are. When the dog is capable of gaiting across the cavalletti numerous times from both directions, end the session and go do something else.

The next time you take the dog out to work the cavalletti, move the pipes 1/2 inch to 1 inch farther apart from each other. The distance depends on the size of your breed—for Toy breeds, increase by 1/2 inch – for larger breeds, increase by 1 inch. Do not move the pipes more than 1 inch apart per session. Again, after the dog is totally comfortable with gaiting over the cavalletti numerous times, end the session and go do something else.

Each time you work the dog, move the pipes the same distance apart as you did in the previous session.

When you reach a distance that the dog cannot do without touching a pipe or without displaying increased resistance or frustration, stop. Put the dog away, move the pipes back to the prior distance, and get the dog. Then start gaiting the dog across the cavalletti again, so that the dog ends the session on a positive note. This is the farthest distance allowed by the dog's structure and is therefore the appropriate distance for cavalletti conditioning.

Do cavalletti sessions 2 or 3 times per week, gaiting the dog across the cavalletti at least 5 or 6 times per session. You can do a session every day, but such frequency is unnecessary.

In addition to building muscles that increase dogs' reach and drive, cavalletti conditioning will convince them to synchronize their legs when gaiting; this enhances smoothness of motion. A dog cannot go across these pipes unless all four legs are working in perfect synchronicity. After only a few sessions, you will see a major improvement in motion. Be aware, however, that if you discontinue this conditioning routine, the dog's motion will go back to what it was before you started.

Cavalletti conditioning is also an excellent way to rehabilitate dogs after they have fully healed from leg injuries. In order to gait the cavalletti effectively, a dog has to bear equal weight on each leg.

GOING OVER A DOG

Many exhibitors have asked me how I, as a judge, go over a dog in the ring. I apply the same procedure that I use when evaluating adult dogs:

First, I step back and look at the picture to determine if the silhouette is the proper picture of the breed. I check the proportions, both height to length and depth of body to length of leg to determine if these are these correct for the breed.

I visualize a line through the topline (following the horizontal) all the way forward to determine if the entire head (chin and all) is above that line.

I visualize a line up the front leg to above the dog to determine if the entire neck and head are in front of that line.

I visualize a line from the point of the buttocks (the bone that sticks out below the base of the tail) to the ground to determine if that line drops directly on the tips of the toes.

Then, I assess the topline through to the croup and tailset, the flow of the neck into the withers, the angle of the pasterns, the height of the hocks, the stifle angle, etc, to determine if the particulars are correct for the breed.

Figure 6-13: Dog with balance lines overlaid
(courtesy of Mikron)

The hands-on portion of the examination starts after I walk to the front of the dog, still standing far enough away to see its head, expression, feet and front assembly. I always speak to dogs I'm going to examine before I touch them, and then I reach for the head.

Once you put a hand on the dog, **do not** break the touch until after you've finished your examination. This will help keep the dog comfortable with your presence and your examination. Removing your hand and then resuming your touch from another direction can cause some dogs to react, which is an unnecessary impediment to the dog, to you and to the examination process. Never do anything to upset the dog and ***never push it***. If the dog resists what you are doing, ease up and try another tactic.

I examine the head first, and the way you do this must be breed specific. Some breed standards call for particular measurements, shapes, proportions, etc. Examine as required by the standard.

I find it very helpful to put a finger or two in the V-shaped indentation under the jaw. This gently encourages most dogs to hold still.

I then examine the bite and mouth. Again, this is breed specific. If the exhibitors want to show the mouth, that's fine. However, I prefer to do it myself. Checking the mouth and bite is usually faster, more accurate and less stressful to the dog if done by those who know what they're doing.

I then move to the side of the dog, while my left hand is still under the chin, and put my right hand in the indentations behind each ear. From this position, I look at head planes. I run my left hand down the front of the neck to check for a ewe neck and then down to the prosternum to check both for muscle-attachment surface and for the proportion of shoulder blade to upper arm. From there, I move my left hand farther underneath to check for the fill of the chest.

While my left hand is still on the dog, I run my right hand down the back of the neck, checking for arch, muscling and width as it approaches the shoulders.

At the shoulders I check for layback, width, fit and smoothness. On coated breeds, I am also looking for a lack of wrinkles over the shoulders. At this point, I push very slightly on the side of the shoulder to check for the stability of the elbows.

While my right hand is still on the dog, I use my left hand to check the underline for the depth and also for any indication of a herring gut.

As I am moving to the rear of the dog, I check the shape of the ribs; I run my thumb down the length of the spine and, with my left hand, actually measure the length of the loin while comparing it to the length of the ribs as viewed from above the dog.

I then run my hands down the front of the rear leg to check the stifle angle, the proper flow of the stifle joint and the proportion of the upper and lower thighs. Next I check the hocks for any motion (if they move inward, the dog is cow-hocked; if they move outward, the dog is barrel- or open-hocked; if they fall forward, the dog has slipped hocks).

I then run my hand up the back edge of the rear leg to check for a balance of tendon attachment and muscle mass and for muscle condition.

With a docked tail, I tickle the underside so the dog will put it up, and on a long tail, I check the full length of the tail for deformities and for length. On both types of tails, I check the actual croup with my palm.

Finally, I step back and check how all of the pieces fit and flow together when viewed from the rear.

Every bit of this examination can be done in less than 30 seconds.

Good judges don't make anything an issue during the examination, so they cause no embarrassment to the exhibitor and no discomfort to the dog. The key elements are soft hands, swiftness and a belief in what your hands and fingertips tell you.

MISCELLANEOUS POINTS

❖ **About stacking and showing:** Most people have difficulty stacking the front legs far enough under the dog; all of us have a tendency to stack the front legs too far forward (and many show photographers encourage it). There is a simple solution. Hold the lead in your right hand, cup your left hand against the dog's left upper arm (the edge of your hand should be at the dog's leg joint), bend the upper arm, and let the leg fall gently in a normal fashion. The leg will set down where it should be. Then simply fix the dog's right leg in alignment with the left. This sets an appropriate stacking pattern for the dog.

Never back a dog up in the show ring. Dogs always move cow-hocked when they are backed up, so it will only succeed in showing the judge a fault the dog may not actually possess.

The only way to ensure that you're not showing off your dog's faults to a judge is to learn what your dog's faults are. This enables you to show the dog in ways that emphasize its strengths and de-emphasize its weaknesses.

When you are in the ring, keep in mind that if your dogs give the impression that being a show dog is their idea (rather than yours), they will give a greater showing.

Figure 6-14: Stacking front legs
(courtesy of Mary Strom)

❖ **About baiting:** We generally had greater success teaching dogs to bait off-lead. Dogs are only given bait when they have done something for it; this way, they learn that bait is something to be earned, unlike food or treats. Use only a type of bait that the dog wants; otherwise, you'll find you are teaching the dog to refuse things. When we have correctly used liver bait, every dog we have handled or worked with has been enthusiastic and done well on it (see Chapter 5, p 91-92). Of course, there are always exceptions to every rule, but the odds are good that liver bait will succeed for you.

Bait is given only when dogs do something for it, and bait is only given in *very* small portions. It is used to reinforce a dog's behavior when it meets the expectations of the exhibitor, so remember to practice only what brings about the desired results. And never tease your dog with an empty hand. Your dog must always be able to trust you and believe in you.

Throughout the teaching process, use a tidbit of bait to reinforce the dog's positive response to every command—every time. After appropriate behavior has been established, switch to a variable reinforcement approach; that is, the dog gets a reward of bait part of the time, but continues to receive praise all of the time. If the dog's behavior backslides at any point, return to constant rewards until the behavior is back on track.

The feet follow the nose. To create the best picture of the dog's front, bait from the front. Baiting from the side teaches the dog to turn out his or her right front foot. Also (and I've no idea why this works), if you hold your bait with both hands, the dog stands still. When you separate your hands, the dog moves.

The appearance of a show dog is created by the head and neck carriage. If you let the dog chew on the bait you're holding, it diminishes the show appearance. Use a large piece of bait that the dog can see; tear off tiny pieces and give them to the dog, but never let the dog reach for a piece.

Avoid carrying bait in your hand while moving the dog around the ring. Bait in hand may wrongly encourage your dog to sidewind. Put the bait in your pocket; show the dog that it is no longer in your hand and then off you go. When the dog has done what you have asked, bait immediately, using only a tidbit from the large piece. Bait is meant to be a reward, not a meal.

❖ **Learn to guesstimate a dog's size with the use of convenient items.** For instance, know the measurement from the ground to your own fingertips at your side (mine is 26 inches), your open hand from tip of thumb to tip of little finger (mine is 8 inches), the height of your fist (mine is 2-3/4 inches), the height of a normal chair seat, the height of a normal banquet table, the ring ropes, etc. Knowing these measurements helps when you are evaluating dogs.

❖ **Don't ever pick up a dog by its mid-section while in the ring, unless your breed is meant to have a roached topline.** Lifting a dog by its mid-section will always create the illusion of a roached topline.

❖ **Dogs naturally oppose force.** If you push, they push back. If you hold their heads up via the collar or lead, you are teaching them to drop their heads. If your dogs lean against you and you allow it or push them away, you're actually teaching them to lean. Opposing force almost always backfires. The trick is to teach them to do what you expect instead of forcing them to do what you want.

❖ **Don't pick a dog up by its tail.** You may see a lot of people doing this, but that doesn't make it right. The tail is an extension of the spine and is used by Terrier people to pull a dog out of burrows. That's fine, since they are pulling in line with the spine. To lift the weight of a dog up by its tail is pulling contrary to the line of the spinal column and could dislocate a vertebrae, causing paralysis. Why take an unnecessary risk?

❖ **To give your dog the best advantage in the ring, always lead it through a stretching exercise before showing.** A Figure 8 works well.

❖ **When a judge is going over your dog, hold its head forward and in proper height.** A turned head will make the dog's shoulders look rougher than what they really are. If the head is held too high, the shoulders will widen. If the head is too low, the shoulders will tighten.

❖ **Keep your hands away from any faults you know of on your dog; the judge's eye will be drawn to where your hands are.**

❖ **The dog's head controls the dog's body.** If the dog moves its head, the dog's legs will move. Keep the head still and the legs will keep still.

❖ **The better a dog is made, the more comfortably it stands still**. The more you touch your dogs when showing, the faultier you make them look.

❖ **Know the terms:** Static balance is the balance of a dog when motionless. Kinetic balance is the balance of the dog in motion. Sprain is a stretched or torn ligament. Strain is a stretched or torn muscle or tendon.

❖ **Muscles don't move; they flex (shorten) or extend (lengthen).**

❖ **If something about a dog's soundness is wrong, something is causing it.**

❖ **"Racking" or "A-framing" (pulling back without moving front feet) can be caused by pasterns that are too straight or too firm.** Walking the dog in loose sand helps to stretch the tissue safely.

❖ **A permanent arch in a topline is inflexible, so it is a serious fault for fast dogs.** A topline must always be flexible.

❖ **A tall, narrow dog is less stable and therefore needs to slow down to make turns.**

❖ **Upper arms provide the proper pendulum motion in a dog's front legs.** Short upper arms change the dog's center of gravity and can cause upright pasterns or knuckling over. Also, short upper arms increase the risk of elbow injuries.

❖ **"Daisy clipping" means you can see the pads of the front feet when the dog is gaiting toward you.** The term comes from the idea of a dog knocking off the tops of flowers when trotting through a field. Daisy clipping is undesirable, as it is a wasted motion; the foot hits the ground heel-pad first instead of full footed and this causes a clumsy gait. It should not be confused with a "low and skimming" step.

❖ **A short neck can cause a lack of balance when the dog is running, jumping and turning.**

❖ **A long neck (within reason) gives a dog several advantages.** A long neck means longer neck muscles, which have greater endurance and quicker responsiveness than short heavy muscles. A long neck aids in locomotion by shifting the center of gravity or balance point of the dog forward, which means more efficient forward motion.

❖ **Upright shoulders create more concussion on the joints.** Thus, a dog with upright shoulders is more likely to suffer shoulder injuries and/or arthritis in its shoulders.

❖ **The straighter and/or higher the shoulder, the higher the dog will have to jump in both Obedience and Agility.**

❖ **Dogs with overangulated rears carry their weight on their toes instead of on their heel pads.**

❖ **Dogs should stand over their front assemblies, not behind them.**

❖ **Efficiency is created by the ability to move in a straight line.** A dog with too long of a loin is incapable of a straight forward motion. (Watch the hair move or bounce over the loin when a dog with too long of a loin is gaiting.) It would be like you walking sideways or hopping for a couple of blocks. You're going to be more tired than if you simply walked those two blocks.

❖ **A dog that breaks stride when moving at a steady trot is a dog with a structural problem.**

❖ **Dogs are supposed to have four toes on each foot and each toe is supposed to carry equal weight.** When a dog has short toes that do not reach the ground, the remaining toes are carrying more of the load than they were intended to, thus they will be more susceptible to injury.

❖ **You can sacrifice type for soundness, but never sacrifice soundness for type.** To do so would be to strive against nature and your breed's best interests.

❖ **It is counterproductive to the dog world for us to award dogs for being right for the wrong reasons.** If this statement leaves you scratching your head, go back and re-read "Structural Review" at the start of this chapter!

*Be prepared: You never get a second chance
to make a first impression.*

grooming for show and health

The more a dog has the look of a show dog, the greater its chances of winning. Moreover, since grooming is an integral part of maintaining a dog's health, it may help to prevent or at least minimize unnecessary problems. For these reasons, grooming is an essential element not only in the sport of purebred dogs but also in the ownership of any dog.

Anyone who is a judge or anyone who wants to be a judge needs to know what can be accomplished with great grooming. It is my belief that grooming should be part of a judge's education—that a Poodle judge should at least know the names of the various coat patterns and a Terrier judge should be familiar with the process of coat stripping and what is involved in maintaining a hard-coated Terrier.

I also believe that the best-groomed dogs at a dog show should be the Obedience and Agility dogs. The Obedience and Agility dogs are, after all, the ones the public watches. When the public approaches those rings, what do they see? Oftentimes, they see dogs so lacking in presentation as to do a disservice to the breeds those dogs represent.

Breeders can do so much to help and teach Obedience and Agility exhibitors how to properly groom the dogs they are going to show. When these exhibitors invest more in the presentation of their dogs, they invest more in the presentation of themselves in the ring, which raises their status in the show world.

ATTENTION TO THE BASICS

For shows, you and the dog need to look the part, be it in Conformation, Obedience or Agility. We are the custodians of our sport, and the public should be able to look to us for guidance by example. We are the ones who can educate, inform and enlighten the public, and the impression we make at shows and exhibitions can work for or against the dog world as a whole.

Nail Care

One of the worst things we can do is neglect our dogs' nails. If you want to know what long nails on a dog's feet feel like, let your nails grow past your fingertips, then go pull weeds by hand for a few hours. Or let your toenails grow to where they press against the inside of your shoes. As a dog's nails begin to bear down on the ground, the dog's foot will stretch, spread or turn to avoid the discomfort. Prolonged neglect may result in the tendons of the feet stretching to such an extent that the foot flattens. The damage is irreparable. No dog should have to endure this avoidable structural harm.

Very few dogs resent having their nails done. What they resent is the fight over nail care. So, don't fight them. Put them on a grooming table, with a noose securely around the base of their head, and stack them comfortably. Then, do the nails. If the dogs fight, don't fight back. Stop and reposition them, then start again. When they realize you aren't going to fight with them, they will usually settle down. (A severe structural weakness or injury is the most common exception to this rule.)

I am a firm believer in grinding nails, as opposed to cutting nails. When grinding, it is better to use the sandpaper cylinders rather than a stone. Stones can get very hot and subsequently cause discomfort. Using the finest grit of sanding bands will eliminate bouncing and reduce vibration against the dog's foot. If done correctly, grinding can actually help train a nail shorter, so each time you grind the nails, you can grind them back a little farther. Cutting the nails way back, on the other hand, can risk an infection in the toe bone.

The bottom of a dog's nail looks like the bottom of a horse's hoof. It has a fleshy center (the sole), a protective ridge (the wall) all the way around the sole, and somewhere in or near the center of the sole is the quick, which is the blood supply conduit.

The only way to encourage a dog's nails to recede is to use a grinder to take back the protective wall of the nail from underneath, until the bottom of the nail is smooth as glass. Doing this nearly exposes the sole (but not to the point of hurting the dog), which then will recede every time something (eg, grass, dirt, gravel) touches it. Each time you grind the nails after that, you will generally be able to take more of the length back.

Figure 7-01: Dog nail from underside

In order to train nails back, all of the nails need to be done from the rear of the leg. When you work on the dog's hind foot, hold the leg straight back. Holding the leg out to the side can cause discomfort, and the dog will resist. Grind down the underside of each nail until it is smooth. Then, grind the length of it in a straight line to the edge of the sole, rounding it if you prefer.

Avoid struggling. Remember, manhandling will make matters worse by encouraging the dog to resort to panic. A helping hand can be useful to support the dog or to help limit resistance, but forcibly holding the dog in place will prolong the struggle.

A colleague who presents an excellent handling seminar around the country believes clipping the nails is preferable to grinding. What fascinates me about this is that his reason is exactly the same as my reason for using a grinder—a prime example of why people should do what works for them.

The best approach is to start familiarizing the dog with nail care when it is very young, while you still have the advantage.

If your dogs resist nail care, remember sometimes things that are good for all of us may feel less than pleasurable. It doesn't mean you should not do them, though. If a child hates getting shots, do we let them go unvaccinated? You owe it to your show dogs to keep them in good condition, right down to their toes.

Bathing

The fundamentals of a great show coat are: (1) genetics, (2) appropriate food and (3) correct coat work and cleaning. Dirt and build-up can damage a dog's coat, so bathing is a necessary element in the care we give our dogs.

One of the most important elements of bathing show dogs, no matter what the breed, is to wash them with free-flowing water. Water shooting out of any kind of nozzle can twist and damage hair on a coated dog and reduce the natural oils in a smooth-coated dog's skin.

Use only dog shampoo, and be sure to dilute it according to the directions. The pH balance of dogs is different than that of humans, so using a human shampoo can adversely affect the dog's coat and skin.

The way I used to test shampoos when my husband and I were handling was to first wash the motor home with the shampoo. It was the easiest way to find out how well it cut grease and grime, how easily it rinsed, what kind of a film it left and what kind of damage it did to my hands after being in it for an hour or so. I'm sure that practice still works well.

Insofar as conditioners are concerned, don't use one unless the dog's coat needs it. There seems to be no single conditioner that is right for all coat types and coat conditions. The best thing to do is to talk with your peers—particularly those whose dogs have the best coats—to find out what works for them. Be careful not to add too much oil to the coat, as oil attracts dirt and dirt is one of the most damaging elements to a dog's coat.

When bathing a show dog, it is very important to learn to wash only the hair. Unless the dog has a specific skin disorder, the skin should be left alone in the bathing process. Dogs need their natural oils to maintain good coat condition. When we scrub a dog's skin, like we scrub our scalps, the natural oils are stripped away.

You can bathe a dog every day of its life without damaging the coat, as long as you bathe the coat and leave the skin alone. Removing a healthy dog's necessary oils from its skin on a regular basis will impair the health of the skin and coat.

Always bathe a show dog with the lay of the hair. Moreover, never pour shampoo along the topline. It may collect in the hair follicles, making it very difficult to rinse out completely. The dog may appear to have dandruff after a day or two, but it is actually the dried shampoo coming loose from the follicles.

For a smooth-coated dog, pour your shampoo onto a dampened net body sponge (the kind used with liquid body soaps for humans) or a regular sponge, then brush the sponge over the coat with the lay of the hair. For a coated dog, pick the hair up in your hand and pour the shampoo onto the hair.

Avoid scouring the hair; use the palm of your hand instead of your fingers. With long hair, knead the shampoo in as if you were washing a fine sweater. Rinse with the lay of the hair. When you rinse, be sure to rinse out all of the soap—you cannot rinse too much. Finally, towel-dry with the lay of the hair.

Dryers

When it comes to dryers, you must have a stand dryer if you have breeds with drop coats (eg, Bearded Collies, Afghans, Malteses). Stand dryers are expensive, but with these kinds of breeds, you have no choice if you want specials-quality hair. It takes two hands to properly dry hair that hangs; this doesn't leave a hand free with which to hold a dryer. With other coated breeds (eg, Golden Retrievers, Belgian Sheepdogs, Siberian Huskies, Pomeranians), you can get by with a forced-air or hand-held dryer. However, stand dryers are the best option and worth every penny you pay for them.

COAT CARE

The trick to great grooming (with the possible exception of Poodles and Bichons) is to make the hair look like God grew it that way. All grooming should be done on a table in front of a mirror, so you have the view of what the judge is going to see.

For proper coat care, it's imperative to use the right tools on the right coats. The tools we will discuss in the following sections are:

- ❖ Pin brush.
- ❖ Slicker.
- ❖ Stainless steel comb.

Figure 7-02: Rake (above), pin brush, slicker, stainless steel comb and blade brush

Figure 7-03: Pumice stone, Mars Coat King (above); rubber fingers and assorted stripping knives

- ❖ Blade brush.
- ❖ Rake.
- ❖ Rubber fingers.
- ❖ Stripping knives.
- ❖ Pumice stone.

About Dog Hair

Perhaps you have heard a term used by Terrier people: "Rolling the coat." This means to remove a portion of the dog's coat on a regular basis. When rolling a coat, Terrier people pull the longest hairs on a continual basis, so that new coat is always coming in. In this way, Terriers can be kept in show coat all year round. If done regularly, a show Terrier will have many levels of coat at any given time—the longest hair ready to be pulled, the medium length in its prime and the shortest length or the new coat emerging.

In many respects, this process applies to all breeds. Each hair follicle holds only one guard hair (ie, hair). It may contain up to thousands of undercoat hairs (ie, fur) but only one guard hair. There is nothing you can do, shy of drugs or spaying/neutering, that will prevent a dog from blowing its undercoat (if it has one). However, you can control the blowing of the top coat or guard hairs. If the guard hair is kept thick and healthy, you can keep almost all dogs in show condition, even when the dogs are blowing their undercoat.

Dog hair grows in cycles, while human hair grows continuously. Except for a few hairs that are constantly falling out in our houses, the dead guard hairs stay in their respective follicles until a new cycle begins. The new growth pushes the old hair out. The natural shedding process will leave a dog out of show condition until the new coat comes in. This is the process you can control.

When hair dies, it loses both its shine and intensity of color. Therefore, if you learn to remove the dead hair regularly, the coat will retain its shine and deeper color, without having to use any cosmetic enhancers. The more products you put on hair, the more hair is damaged and the faster it dies.

Since new hair pushes out the old hair as it surfaces, dead hair stays in place, waiting for the next cycle. However, when you remove dead hair before it is ready to shed naturally, new growth is immediately stimulated. Thus, the more dead hair you remove in regular grooming sessions, the more new growth is constantly in progress and the greater the chances of the dog remaining in show condition.

Each type of coat needs to be "rolled" in a different fashion.

Drop-Coated Breeds

The first required tool for drop-coated breeds is a pin brush. Make sure the pin brush you use has metal pins in a rubber base. Plastic and nylon cause static, and static breaks hair. Use brushes with metal bristles only, and no knobs on the ends of the bristles. The more flexible the side motion of the bristles, the less damage it will cause to the hair.

For breeds requiring brushing, you will also have need of a slicker. The slicker is used on all feet up to the stop pad on the front legs and up to the hock joint on the rear legs. Foot hair is a different texture than the rest of the coat and is more effectively separated with a slicker than with a pin brush. I have found that a long-handled, smaller slicker is preferable because it has better balance, which encourages proper use.

Teach the dog to lie down on the table. This means you must lay the dog in the position you want, as opposed to the position the dog might want (for example, the dog may want to lay in such a way as to hide an area it doesn't want you to brush). Stand the dog on the table, embrace it around the far elbow and knee, draw the dog into your body and then lay it gently on its side, keeping your body on the dog until it relaxes in this position.

Figure 7-04: Shih Tzu

Figure 7-05: Yorkshire Terrier

Figure 7-06: Afghan Hound

Laying the dog on the table to brush it is the only way you can keep a long-coated dog in great show coat. Every hair needs to be brushed against the lay of the coat. This is the only way to remove dead hair before it is ready to fall out, and removing dead hair stimulates new growth. If you brush with the lay of the hair, you will only be removing hair that has already begun shedding. Brushing against the lay of the coat is problematic if the dog is standing. You'll find yourself brushing against gravity, which will tire your arm quickly and make for a less than thorough job.

Never brush hair that is dry, since this will cause static and static breaks hair. Also, laying a dog down on a carpeted surface to brush it can pull static from the carpet into the coat. Always mist the hair before brushing it. Brush wet hair only when using a dryer on it. Wet hair stretches and weakens when brushed, but brushing with a dryer relieves the tension on the hair.

Mist over the coat with water or whatever you find works best for your breed, then line-brush the coat (make a line at the skin and brush one line of hair at a time) lightly enough that you do not hear the brush going through the coat. Remember, every hair is brushed against the lay. Keep the motion in the wrist, and brush the hair from the skin all the way to the end of the hair.

After you have brushed every hair against the lay, stand the dog up and brush the coat again—this time, in the pattern appropriate for the breed. You may also go through the coat at this stage with a stainless steel comb to ensure all loose hair has been removed.

Figure 7-07: Line brushing

When using a comb, put it into the coat perpendicular to the body. Putting a comb into the coat at an angle can tear out hair. Use a slicker on the dog's feet and on all short-coated areas (always against the lay first).

One of the easiest ways to remove mats with the least amount of damage to the coat is to use a slicker. Put your hand between the mat and the dog's skin. Push the slicker down into the mat until the slicker's pins rest on your hand. Then move the slicker around in a circular scrubbing motion, both clockwise and counterclockwise, to break up the mat. Gently lift the slicker out of the mat and then use your fingers to separate the matted hair. Only when the hair is separated do you brush through the mat with a pin brush.

Powder the coat in areas where something is caught in the hair, be it seeds, twigs or brambles. Baby powder works well. The powder will coat whatever is stuck in the hair, and then you can brush through that area without ripping or damaging hair. If there is urine in the coat, the best option is to bathe that area before brushing it, but powdering it does help. In fact, keeping males regularly powdered underneath can help to prevent urine from sticking to the coat in the first place.

Smooth-Coated Breeds

All it takes to keep a smooth-coated dog's coat in show condition is a chamois and a pumice stone. A pumice stone, used lightly with the lay of

Figure 7-08: Dalmatian

Figure 7-09: Great Dane

Figure 7-10: Doberman Pinscher

the hair, will remove the dead hair in the same fashion that brushing a coated breed against the lay does.

When using a pumice stone, scrape the sharp edges along a hard surface first to round them off. Run the stone along the coat in a rolling fashion to avoid cutting any of the hair. Applying pressure is unnecessary. Make sure the skin is pulled taut over any area where the skin is normally wrinkled, plump or loose.

"Stoning" a smooth-coated breed in this fashion once or twice a week keeps the coat lustrous and rich in color, while considerably reducing the amount of shedding the dog does in the house.

After stoning, soak a good-quality chamois in hot water, ring it out well and then wipe down the dog. The chamois removes any residue left from the pumice stone, and the natural oil in the cloth will leave the coat wonderfully shiny, thus eliminating the need for additional products to make the coat look good.

A smooth-coated dog should go into the ring looking smooth; in other words, there should be no hairs jutting out anywhere to disrupt the lines of the dog. Use thinning shears to trim away any such hair.

Never use a clipper on a smooth-coated breed. Clippering a smooth coat thickens the coat and will lighten the color. Furthermore, you run the risk of the new hair coming in curly or wavy. Why risk ruining the coat of perhaps the best dog you ever bred? Learn to care for the coat properly before the wrong approach costs you a Best In Show.

Spitz Breeds

Spitz breeds, such as Samoyeds, Siberian Huskies, Shiba Inus, Keeshonden and Pomeranians, have a dense double coat. The only way to keep such a coat in good condition is to keep it free of loose undercoat and to be constantly removing dead guard hair so that new coat is always coming in.

Every hair must be line-brushed against the lay, as with the drop-coated breeds. However, if the coat is short enough, it can be brushed with a slicker. For longer coats (2 inches or more in length), use a pin brush.

Too many people believe that brushing this type of coat will take out the undercoat, which will make the coat as a whole appear too thin. Actually, just the opposite is the case. The more a Spitz breed is properly brushed, the thicker its coat will be. As a judge, I am appalled when I examine a dog in the show ring that has a matted, packed undercoat. Remember, the welfare of our dogs

Figure 7-11: Alaskan Malamute

Figure 7-12: Keeshond

Figure 7-13: Samoyed

Figure 7-14: Long-Haired Dachshund

Figure 7-15: Papillon

Figure 7-16: Irish Setter

should be our top priority.

Coated Breeds With Jackets

These are the breeds that have hanging hair in some areas, but you want the "jacket," or torso coat, to lie smoothly and tightly over the body. Coated breeds with jackets include Golden Retrievers, Bouviers des Flandres, Setters, Bernese Mountain Dogs, Papillons, Australian Shepherds, the Belgian herding breeds and many more.

For this type of coat, brush all furnishings against the lay, as with drop-coated breeds. Work the jacket with the lay, first using a stripping knife (or a Mars Coat King) as a comb followed by a pumice stone. Both of these steps remove dead hair but at different layers.

Follow this procedure with what is referred to as "packing the coat." For this step, you will need a blade brush (or a dense, natural-bristle brush on which all the bristles are the same length). There should be very little space between the rows of bristles, and the bristle surface must be level. A level surface is required for flattening and straightening the coat—any curve to the bristle surface will lift the coat.

Along with a blade brush, you will need a spray bottle of water (for coats that are bathed) or a spray bottle of rubbing alcohol (for jacketed coats that are pulled and not bathed) and a hand towel easily rolled up in your hand. Using a white towel will help keep you from returning dirt to the coat.

Wet the jacket from the appropriate spray bottle. Then, with the blade brush in one hand and the rolled-up towel in the other, alternate strokes along the lay of the jacket until the coat is completely dry and laying the way you want. Packing the jacket at least twice a week will control even the wildest of hair. Use a slicker on the feet and short-coated areas, and check for loose hair with a comb, just as you would do on a drop-coated breed.

Hard-Coated Breeds (Wire or Broken)

For any hair that must be pulled, you will need rubber fingers, stripping knives, a Dr. Scholl's Corn and Callous Remover and a pumice stone. If you are a serious Terrier person, you may learn to pull hair almost entirely with your bare fingers, but beware the price your body may have to pay as you get older. Rubber fingers give you better traction, so you don't have to work as hard to pull hair, which makes the process easier on your hands, arms and elbows. Another easy assist is to sprinkle the

Figure 7-17: Wire-Haired Dachshund

Figure 7-18: Giant Schnauzer

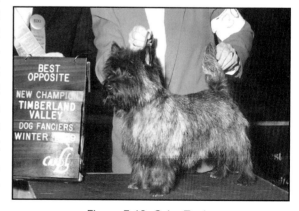

Figure 7-19: Cairn Terrier

coat with R-7 Ear Powder. This product contains rosin, which also provides traction and makes the hair easier to manipulate.

There are many types of stripping knives of varying functions available for stripping wire or broken coats. Check with your breed mentors to learn which knives are best for your breed and its coat type. When you are pulling other coats, use a selection of knives. If you have a variety of knives available, you can switch back and forth, which will save your hand unnecessary strain and soreness.

When you are learning how to pull hair, I recommend using a Dr. Scholl's Corn and Callous Remover instead of a stripping knife. You are less likely to cut hair with this tool. When you get proficient, and then buy your stripping knives.

The pumice stone is used to remove dead hair; it is used like a brush. Very little pressure is needed; just brush over the coat lightly (with the lay). You can then comb through the coat with a small-toothed stripping knife to remove undercoat. Done on a regular basis (once a week), this will help keep the coat in a steady state of growth and rejuvenation.

SCISSORING

With regard to scissoring, you must learn how to pick up scissors so that as you cut, only one blade is moving. This enables you to cut straighter lines. Put your little finger under the finger rest; put the next finger in the finger hole; then put the next two fingers under the edge of the scissors for balance. Your thumb slips into the thumbhole.

Figure 7-20: Correct hold on scissors

When you hold scissors in this manner only the thumb moves, so only one blade moves. Make sure to keep just the tips of your finger and thumb in the holes, otherwise your hand loses leverage.

Handle scissors in order to know if they fit, because every pair fits a hand differently. Also, while learning to scissor, use average-quality scissors.

With average quality, you have more chances to scissor over mistakes. With high-quality scissors, one chance to cut right is all you get. As you improve, improve the quality of the scissors you buy.

As for thinning shears, it is best to get a pair that only has teeth on one of the blades. Double-sided thinning shears can cut chunks. Also, the fewer number of teeth on the shears (or a coarse cutting blade) will create a finer finish. Most thinning shears have approximately 44 teeth. I recommend a 32-tooth shear. The more teeth there are the more scissor marks you will leave on the coat. A 32-tooth shear takes more cutting time, but it leaves considerably fewer marks.

Keep a chunk of white chalk with your scissors. The chalk absorbs moisture, so your scissors will stay sharp longer.

SHOW TIPS

Keep in mind that the objective is to make most breeds look like nature has created perfection rather than grooming has created the illusion of perfection.

❖ **Buy only nylon nooses for your grooming arm.** Leather nooses can leave a dye ring on a wet dog. Flat-ribbed nooses are my favorite, since they seem to be more comfortable for the dog.

❖ **Refrain from clippering whiskers on a dog with a dark face, because clippering whiskers can make the dog's muzzle gray faster.** On dark faces, use only scissors to remove whiskers, if you want to remove them. I don't believe any dog has ever won or lost on the status of its whiskers; however, make sure to check your breed standard to verify that removing whiskers is an acceptable practice.

❖ **If your dogs are prone to tarter buildup and nothing you've tried has helped, note that there is a hot wax treatment available for your dog's teeth.** It's called ProVseal. Check it out on the Web, and ask your vet about it the next time you have your dog's teeth cleaned.

❖ **A word about chalks:** It is legal to use chalks as long as you are using them for cleaning purposes, and you remove the chalk before showing. One of the best formulas is one-half cornstarch, one-quarter baby powder, and one-quarter of any of the commercial grooming powders. Cornstarch alone does not stick to hair; baby powder alone is too silky and can be felt in a coat even after removal; commercial powders alone have to be bathed out or they damage the coat. The combination of all three, however, can't be felt, sticks to coat, and does not have to be washed out.

❖ **When bathing a dog that has stains, use only lukewarm water.** Cold or hot water can set stains. To remove grease from a coat, use liquid dish washing soap and cold water. (If the coat is extremely greasy, lather the coat with detergent or shampoo while the coat is dry.) Hot water dissolves the grease to where it soaks into the hair shaft and is still in the coat after you dry the dog. Cold water will bead up the grease so you can wash it off of the hair shaft.

❖ **Crystal White Shampoo by EZ Groom is a great whitening shampoo.** To remove stains, wet a white washcloth or hand towel, pour some Crystal White Shampoo on the wet cloth and heat it in the microwave. Take it out and wave it in the air until it cools to a tolerable temperature for the dog. Wrap the stained area in this towel for 5 to 10 minutes and then bathe as usual.

❖ **Boric acid powder, either dry or mixed with water to make a paste, can be used to remove stains.** It is particularly helpful in keeping face hair white and stain free.

❖ **If you are having problems with severe static, Static Guard, or water mixed with a small measure of liquid fabric softener, sprayed lightly on your brush may help.** Also, a satin crate pad cover eliminates most static.

❖ **Oil can be very damaging to hair if applied to a coat improperly.** Oil treatments are not for novice show groomers.

❖ **Practice your brushing technique.** The closer to the end of a brush handle you can hold a brush, the better job of brushing you will do.

❖ **Hair that is scissored tends to separate when the dog moves.** Hair that is pulled tends to cling to the surrounding hair.

❖ **When pulling hair, pull in the direction you want the hair to grow.** Pulling can affect the direction hair grows by turning the follicle in the direction you're pulling.

❖ **Try to work only the undercoat when attempting some "creative grooming."** Trying to hide anything about the dog by manipulating its top coat may actually draw attention to what you're trying to make unnoticeable.

❖ **Straggly hairs give the dog the appearance of being thin-coated.** Short and thick is better than long and straggly.

❖ **Always take nails back as far as possible before scissoring feet, then scissor only to the end of the nail.** If the nails show, the foot will give the appearance of being longer and flatter than it is.

❖ **Except on Poodles and any other breeds that are supposed to have shaved feet, never scissor between toes from underneath, since this can adversely affect the tight look of the foot from the top.** If the toes look separated, the foot will give the appearance of being flatter than it is.

❖ **If your breed standard allows it, remove the hair from around the large pad of the foot.** If that hair accumulates such things as mud, snow, feces, urine, etc, it can break the foot down.

❖ **Blue shampoo intensifies yellow stains.** Purple shampoo neutralizes yellowing.

Remember that grooming is an act of preventive health care, as well as a necessary piece of the whole package. Our first responsibility is to the health and well-being of our dogs. If we meet that responsibility, we enhance more than their show appearances.

It makes no difference what you name your cat—
It never comes when you call it anyway.

---

advertising dogs

Rick Rutledge was the original owner of *Canine Chronicle*, the first weekly dog show magazine. The *Chronicle* had been in circulation for a year or two, when the AKC board asked for Rick's attendance at one of their board meetings. At the meeting, the board said something to the effect that it disapproved of the *Chronicle*; they felt that it served only to attempt to influence AKC's judges.

This is one of those moments where a normal person thinks of a pithy reply a week after the fact. Rick told me later that he had no idea how his reply sprang to mind right there and then. He said to the board, "Gentlemen, if your judges judged dogs, I'd be out of business tomorrow."

The meeting ended, and the board never said another word about it to him. And Rick was right. No one would spend money on advertising if it didn't help. Therein lies the credence in the saying: "It pays to advertise." Considering the number and sizes of the all-breed publications available, it really must be true.

TARGET THE AUDIENCE

When advertising, first decide who you want to reach. It is the cornerstone of any advertising campaign—targeting the audience. Advertising is a waste of money and effort if it never comes to the attention of the right people.

If you are advertising stud dogs or are trying to become a recognizable name in your breed (or at least an impressive presence among your peers), stick with breed publications. If you are advertising for the sole purpose of selling puppies, be sure to advertise where new buyers are looking. One effective avenue is breeder websites. This option puts you and your dogs right out there for the public at large to find. I prefer the websites that include the pros and cons of owning the breed in question, as well as straightforward information about necessary care and training. However, prospective puppy buyers should know that less than reputable breeders can make their dogs look really good on a website; breeders should know that prospective Internet puppy buyers may be more difficult to screen.

Breed-specific publications are great magazines. However, people who are new to the world of purebred dogs and shows are unaware of the existence of these publications (although the presence of the Internet in more people's home may be changing this). Therefore, unless you are a recognizable name in your breed, you probably will have less success in selling puppies through breed publications.

A moment of editorializing, if you will permit me: AKC, to the public, means quality. If AKC is going to maintain that reputation, it needs to do all in its power to prevent puppy mills from advertising in the *Gazette*. The effort is there. As I understand it, for instance, the *Gazette* will not accept ads from any USDA-licensed breeders. However, the AKC needs our help to stay on top of the situation. If you ever find a breeder's classified ad in the *Gazette* to be suspect, contact the publication directly. *Dog World* and *Dog Fancy* classified ads may very well include a high percentage of puppy mills. It would be a shame should the *AKC Gazette* develop that type of customer base.

Keep in mind that the AKC is only a registration body; it is not a police force. It has no right to refuse registration to any proven purebred puppies. On the other hand, the *AKC Gazette* has every right to ensure that its advertisers are responsible breeders dedicated to the quality, betterment and well-being of their breeds.

Back to the topic at hand: I believe the main reason for advertising is to try to influence judges (or at least catch their eye). If that is your purpose, place your ads in the publications read by judges. The better the writers and articles, the greater the chances that judges are reading. The all-breed magazines are sent to the majority of the AKC-approved judges. Then again, you can always ask some of your favorite judges which publications they read.

The breed-specific magazines are very important to owners and breeders, but they are probably not the wisest use of your advertising dollars if your purpose is to reach judges.

THE ADVERTISING BUDGET

The same things relevant to smart spending in the care and show preparation of our dogs applies to advertising our dogs. Figure out how much you can afford per year on advertising, and then use that money to your best advantage.

If you buy a new Volvo and drive it off the lot, you are suddenly amazed by the number of Volvos you see on the road. Once we're associated with something, we notice it more.

If you have Akitas, you're going to take notice of all other Akitas you see in show magazines, but you might never notice the ads on Toy breeds. If, however, you open three consecutive issues of a magazine and see an ad for my Maltese in each one, you will most likely remember all of the ads, because the human mind generally remembers something after encountering it three consecutive times. This is known in the advertising world as a "recticular activating system." So the first thing to understand is that ads are most effective if they are run in units of three.

Second, use a different ad each time. If you use the exact same ad over and over, readers will think they've seen it before and pass over it. So use a different ad, but have a theme or similar layout or use the same print style or logo–some characteristic that will immediately identify the ad as yours.

AD LAYOUTS

Layout is paramount to successful advertising. The fewer words in an ad, the more likely it will be read. The more white space in an ad, the more likely it will be looked at. You only want necessary information. The exception is advertising in breed publications; in these ads, there is no such thing as too much information, and the information should always include the names of the sire, dam and breeder.

One of the most important pieces of ad information aimed at judges is the location where the dog is being shown. Take care, however. This piece of information requires subtlety. You want to let judges know in what area of the country the dog is being shown, without giving the impression of pushing your dog on judges' attentions. For example, if you are showing your own dog, provide not only your name (as owner-handler) but your address as well. This will tell judges in an unobtrusive way where your dog is being shown.

Many judges think the tactic of saying specifically where the dog will be shown backfires. For example: "See you in Louisville." It comes across as pushy instead of informative. Trying to shove any portion of an ad down a judge's throat won't make points with your target audience. Advertising should entice, not offend.

Location is significant because advertising is more of an interest catcher than an influence. When I see an ad for a gorgeous Great Dane, for instance, I want to know in what area of the country it's being shown so that I can look for that Dane when I judge in that part of the country. That's not to say I will put the Dane up, but it will get a second look, because I'm keeping an eye out for it. (That's not politics—it's human nature.)

If you prefer, there are companies that specialize in dog show advertising, and they do a great job. Be prepared, though—their services are expensive.

If you want help putting an advertising campaign together or are in the market for business cards or a logo or whatever, go to any local community college or university that has classes in advertising or layout or graphic arts, and meet with the instructor. Offer a prize of $50 or $100 for the student who comes up with the best idea for what you need. That way, you're getting 20 or 30 ideas as opposed to one idea from a company that could charge you as much as $500 for a logo. Students can come up with some great ideas, and most instructors love it because they like their students to work on practical projects.

AD PHOTOS

With ideas for layout in mind, determine what kinds of pictures you are going to use. When you're getting started, you can use informal shots in breed publications, but use only show photos in all-breed show magazines. Most people in this world (not just those in the dog world) are followers. If you want judges to take notice, you need to let them know that the dog is winning under a variety of judges–hence, the sensible use of show photos.

Save your great photos for when your dog is a recognizable name. That is when you want your ads to be the most memorable.

Insofar as photos are concerned, make a copy of the photo you intend to use. It is important to know how it will reproduce in black and white or color and on the type of paper used by the magazine's printers.

Pay attention to what you're wearing when you show your dogs; we always do our best winning when we least expect it, so always be prepared. For black and white ads, avoid wearing red if you have dark-colored dogs, since red reproduces either black or dark gray. Refrain from wearing checks with smooth-coated dogs, because it will distort the topline of the dog in a photo. Forgo wearing patterns or prints with a parti-colored dog, because it will wash out the dog.

Always publish photos that put your dog in the best possible light. In other words, you want to use only photos that show off the dog's structural and breed strengths. Guaranteed, a bad photo will be interpreted as a lousy dog, not a lousy picture.

Never–and I mean absolutely never–alter a photograph in its print form to improve the look or quality of the dog. Ethics and integrity aside, the alteration may look fine as a photograph but will show as an altered photo when reproduced.

Finally, use photos in which all of the participants are looking at the dog. When all eyes are on the dog, the reader's eyes will automatically focus on the dog as well; in photos where the people are looking toward the camera, your eye is first going to focus on the person who is looking back at you (see figures on p 150).

The dog needs to be the center of attention in the ad. You can't always get everyone to look at the dog, but you can ask the photographer to request it of the people in the photo shoot.

ATTENTION TO STRATEGY

You expect too much if you try to advertise a dog into wins.

Figure 8-01: All eyes on the dog
(courtesy of Perry Phillips)

Figure 8-02: All eyes on the camera
(courtesy of Perry Phillips)

Although judges may be intrigued by an ad, they will not be told what to do by advertisements. For instance, most judges have no appreciation for standards quoted in ads.

Stick to advertising only what the dog has already accomplished. While you're building wins, keep your ads simple. Once you have some big wins under your belt, then is the time to advertise big, if you so choose. And keep your ads positive. Negative remarks about one's competition may be an accepted practice in political campaigns, but it is inappropriate when advertising dogs.

Remember to take a soft approach with your ads. You want to entice, not offend. Judges, like all of us, hate having their sensibilities treaded upon. Inform gently—perhaps with a touch of humor or elegance—dazzle with an excellent photo, but don't push.

ADVERTISING REVIEW

1. Determine who your target audience is.

2. Decide where you are going to advertise and how often, in accordance with your budget.

3. Select the right layout for your ad—keep it simple, with a signature characteristic that easily identifies the ad as yours.

4. Select photos that capture the best your dog can be.

No failure is ever final—nor is any success.

the breeder's integrity

Breeding dogs does not necessarily make one a breeder. Being a good breeder involves dedication to the constant improvement of your particular breed of dog.

Planning and protecting the future of your breed is what will make you a breeder. A healthy, sound dog is your top priority and first responsibility as a breeder. Your next responsibility is to breed in accordance with your breed standard–not for what you like or what fashion may be winning at the moment, but for what your standard requires. With the rising lobbies against dog breeding in this country, responsible breeding is the first best hope for staving off the potential onslaught of legislated prohibitions.

Again, to be a good breeder, read your breed standard. Study it, understand it and breed for quality, not quantity. There are enough dogs in the world already. To breed dogs just for selling stock is almost criminal–and I'm not referring to traditional puppy mills.

If you want to be a good breeder, you have to be responsible for the dogs you bring into this world throughout the whole of their lives. You must also make the hard decisions, such as putting puppies down that are incapable of dealing with and living in our world, as well as spaying or neutering dogs that most likely would produce mentally or physically unsound puppies.

With very few exceptions, I am opposed to repeat breedings, because we should always breed for improvement. When we repeat a breeding, all we are doing is duplicating what we've already done. If quality and improvement are not your first concerns in breeding, give up breeding–for the sake of your breed.

Figure 9-01: Sporting Group—English Setter

Figure 9-02: Hound Group—
Scottish Deerhound

I also believe dogs should be bred to fit their breed standards instead of rewriting standards to fit the dogs being bred. Knowing your breed standard is the first best step to breeding or showing. Judging is a subjective activity, and breed standards are open to interpretation, but all of us need parameters within which to begin and proceed in this sport. Breed standards and AKC rules are the fundamentals of our sport. Remember, however, that nothing in our sport is absolute. All you can do is the best you can do for your breed and your sport.

Health and temperament problems are becoming so severe that we must pay more attention to what we're doing and how we're breeding. If we're unwilling to do this, we may have to forfeit the right to breed dogs in this country. If you are having any kind of problem in any aspect of your dogs' genetic health, go to the experts (see the Resources section of this book). Don't try to figure it out with your next-door neighbor or your general-practice veterinarian. Go to those who know the most, the people who are doing the research. None of us can reduce the instances of genetic problems until we learn what they are. Only then can we learn how to deal with these problems—and learn we must.

Research what is acceptable and what is illegal in the enhancing and altering of dogs. Remember the primary objective of Conformation showing is to help determine the best quality for breeding. If you spend time and money fixing the appearance of a dog at the expense of breeding quality, you are simply creating the illusion of quality while propagating the problems you're trying to disguise. That is not what the sport intended, and if you lose sight of the intention, you risk your own integrity as a breeder.

The breeders who know what problems their specific breeds are prone to are the breeders who have fewer problems, because they learn how to prevent them. Problem prevention begins with a thorough knowledge of our dogs. There is no excuse for not knowing your dogs in detail, including such things as the number of teeth, condition of the testicles and range of temperaments in each litter. It is my opinion that if a dog is not equipped to function as a dog, it certainly should not be bred, let alone presented in the show ring. Our responsibility is to breed whole, healthy animals.

The longer you are in dogs, the more you will find value in using an overlay of the physical structure of a dog. All pages in place give you the full structure; lifting each page removes one layer of structure at a time. This is an invaluable tool for the breeder as well as the exhibitor.

Always bear in mind that it is a breeder's responsibility to breed dogs that are capable of doing what they were originally bred to do. If a Herding dog is incapable physically or temperamentally of herding, a Hound or Sporting dog of hunting, a Terrier of going to ground, then that dog should be spayed or neutered. As responsible breeders, however, our first obligation is to do all we can to minimize the chance of bringing such a dog into this world. A conscientious breeder must be dedicated to safeguarding and furthering the physical and mental integrity of purebred dogs.

Also, as breeders it is our responsibility to place dogs in appropriate homes. The dog has to fit its owner's lifestyle and activities. Is it right to sell a puppy with structural weaknesses to a person who wants a dog as a long-distance running companion? It is a bad match for the

Figure 9-03: Working Group—Doberman Pinscher

Figure 9-04: Terrier Group—Scottish Terrier

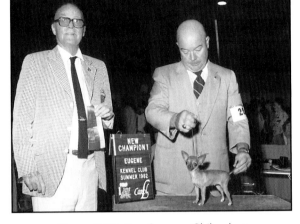

Figure 9-05: Toy Group—Chihuahua

puppy and for the prospective owner.

I am constantly dumbfounded by the number of breeders who think that their "pet" puppies can be sold to performance homes. Homes looking for a dog to work or do performance competitions require dogs with the soundest structure. A dog that falls short of its breed type but has exquisitely sound structure may be the best choice for these homes.

If prospective owners are looking for something that would be found more readily in another breed, suggest that breed and save you, them and your puppies the heartache of a bad match.

Finally, plan your breeding program with care. If you are breeding to make money, you cannot afford to be as careful as you ought to be in developing a breeding program. Breeding is ideally an effort of love and should not be a commercial venture. It is an expensive endeavor, but the return on investment must be in quality, not in capital. Consider your motive before you proceed, and for the sake of the dog world, make sure you are breeding dogs for the right reason.

In your breeding program, then, breed for total quality. The body has to be balanced; balance means all pieces function together as one whole. The dog has to be a good mix of structural soundness and breed-specific capabilities, along with good health and proper type and temperament.

When buyers take one of your puppies home, whether they pay for a show prospect or a pet, their confidence in buying from a breeder instead

Figure 9-06: Non-Sporting Group—Dalmatian

Figure 9-07: Herding Group—Cardigan Welsh Corgi

of from a pet store is in your hands, as are the lives of the dogs your breeding program has produced. It is up to you to help challenge the attitude of people who swear they will only have mixed breeds because there are too many problems that come with a purebred dog.

To each prospective buyer, you represent all breeders. It is a sobering responsibility to carry–puppies and people are depending on your integrity, best intentions and willingness to keep learning.

Ethics and AKC rules

According to an *AKC Bulletin* published in November 1989, the regulations regarding alterations to show dogs come down to this: If you do anything to a dog to alter its appearance from what it might have been if you had not done the alteration, it is illegal.

The best rule you can follow is to breed carefully instead of breeding to whatever and fixing the result. Also, be aware of what surgical procedures are acceptable and unacceptable for show. AKC has established a list of acceptable surgical procedures. It is a good idea to know what they are and the fines and suspensions associated with those procedures that are unacceptable.

Figure 10-01: Golden Retriever—Obedience

Figure 10-02: Newfoundland—Water Trial

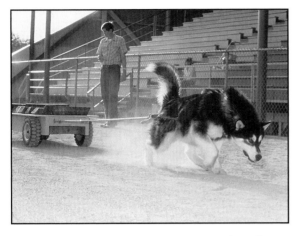

Figure 10-03: Alaskan Malamute—Weight Pulling

Figure 10-04: Labrador Retriever—Water Retrieve

AKC has a rule book for every show event, be it Conformation, Obedience, Den and Herding Trials, or any of the myriad other activities you can get involved in with your dog. A good habit to get into is to always have with you every rule book that applies to every event in which you and your dogs are competing (for rule books and regulations, go to www.akc.org/insideAKC/regs.cfm).

Moreover, keep in mind that AKC does not write the breed standards—parent clubs write breed standards. If you have a problem with your breed's standard, look to your parent club. AKC is not to blame. If you are unhappy with what your parent club does, then get involved and try to make things better. Just complaining about what's wrong never helps anyone, including you.

If you have a measurable or weighable breed (a breed with a height or weight disqualification for conformation), be sure you know the rules, as well as your dog's measurements or weight. There is no excuse for an exhibitor or handler to be ignorant of his or her dog's size.

Know how to measure and weigh your dog correctly. Judges are taught at seminars, but breeders and owners should be the first to know. If you have any questions about measuring or weighing, contact your local AKC representative for assistance.

Both the measuring wickets and the scale must be set by the judge, but make sure you check them yourself.   The dog must be measured in a normal show stance. If you have a breed that is stacked on a table, measuring must take place on the table. If you have a breed that is stacked on the floor, measuring must take place on the floor.

Weighing accurately is more difficult, due to the fact that there is a variety of weighing equipment used.

If a dog is found to be ineligible for its class or division, it must be excused. If the breed standard dictates a disqualification for height or weight and the dog does not fit within the standard, then the dog must be disqualified. A dog that has been disqualified by three different judges may not be shown again.

Know what products and procedures are illegal to use on show dogs. My personal belief is that any product or procedure that alters or masks the genetic foundation of a dog is wrong–period–end of story. The AKC rule is: Any alteration that changes the appearance of a dog makes the dog ineligible for show.

All breed standards override AKC rules. Therefore, it is legal to crop ears, dock tails and remove dewclaws, in accordance with specific breed standards. Some breed standards even allow for honorable scars.

I do not advocate using anything that misrepresents the true genetic makeup of a dog. It cheats the sport and hurts our breeds.

When it comes to AKC rules generally, anyone who is going to show dogs will encounter debate and conflicting views. Know now that interpretations and perceptions will vary. Judges barely have time to judge the dogs; they have no time to police the particular practices of each exhibitor.

Nothing about showing dogs is absolute, and the sooner you understand this, the sooner you can let go of that expectation and enjoy the experience more fully. If you see a specific problem surfacing in your breed, your best option is to raise the issue with your parent club. That's where change can really begin.

As for exhibiting, preparation and presentation choices are yours alone. The choices you make may or may not have negative consequences, but consider this: Those exhibitors who prepare and present their dogs with reasonable honesty and gracious conduct are a credit to the breeds they show, win or lose. And each exhibitor who walks away with a Best In Show award through integrity, hard work and careful breeding enriches the sport and the world of purebred dogs.

PHA and AKC-registered handler Randy Schepper has a saying that I truly love and completely agree with: "Show your dog to its best advantage without taking advantage of anybody else." Do what it takes to show your dog in the best possible light—show the judge the best your dog can be. Remember, you paid the same amount for your entry as everyone else. Get your money's worth, but not at someone else's expense.

As members of the sport of purebred dogs, all we can do is the best we can do, and try to share what we know. Be a mentor to beginners coming up behind you. Teach what you can, and keep your mind open to new information. Nothing remains static, so we harm ourselves, our breeds and our sport by standing still.

Thoughtfully advance. Dare to be a good example.

resources

MAGAZINES

AKC Gazette
260 Madison Ave
New York NY 10016-2401
(212) 696-8200
Subscriptions: (800) 533-7323
www.akc.org/pubs

Canine Chronicle
3622 NE Jackson Rd
Ocala FL 34479
(352) 369-1104
www.caninechronicle.com

Dogs in Review
PO Box 15836
North Hollywood CA 91615-5836
(818) 286-3107
www.dogsinreview.com

Dog News
1115 Broadway
New York NY 10010
(212) 807-7100 ext. 588
www.dognews.com

Showsights
8848 Beverly Hills
Lakeland FL 33809-1604
(941) 858-3839
www.dmcg.com/pubs/showsight

ASSOCIATIONS

Owner Handlers Association (OHA)
Rose Robischon
1100 Ridgebury Rd
New Hampton NY 10958
(914) 374-2708
www.prodogs.com/OHA

Professional Handlers Association (PHA)
Kathleen Bowser
17017 Norbrook Dr
Oney MD 20832
(301) 924-0089
www.phadoghandlers.com

Professional Handlers Certification Board (CPH)
Jane Flowers
413 Dempsey Ave, SW
Buffalo MN 55313
(612) 682-3366
www.infodog.com/misc.dhg

American Dog Owners Association (ADOA)
1654 Columbia Turnpike
Castleton NY 12033
www.adoa.com

CANINE HEALTH

Brucellosis
Diagnostic Lab
College of Veterinary Medicine
Cornell University
PO Box 5786
Ithaca NY 14852-5786
(607) 253-3900
FAX: (607) 253-3943

Brucellosis
OSU Veterinary Diagnostic Laboratory
College of Veterinary Medicine
Oregon State University
PO Box 429
Corvallis OR 97339-0429
(541) 737-3261
FAX: (541) 737-6817

Canine Reproduction

Dr. Robert van Hutchinson
Animal Clinic Northview
34910 Center Ridge Rd
North Ridgeville OH 44039
(440) 327-8282
FAX: (440) 353-0331
info@northviewvet.com
www.northviewvet.com

Cardiac Conditions

American College of Veterinary Internal
    Medicine–Cardiology
1997 Wadsworth, Ste A
Lakewood CO 80214-5293
(800) 245-9081
(303) 231-9933
FAX: (303) 231-0880
www.acvim.org

Cardiac Conditions

Dr. David Sisson
Department of Veterinary Clinical Medicine
School of Veterinary Medicine
University of Illinois
1008 W. Hazelwood Dr
Urbana IL 61801
(217) 333-5300
Appointment Hotline: (217) 265-5163
FAX: (217) 244-1475
d-sisson@uiuc.edu

Canine Eye Registration Foundation (CERF)

VMDB/CERF
Purdue University
CERF/Lynn Hall
625 Harrison St
West Lafayette IN 47907-2026
(765) 494-8179
FAX: (765) 494-9918
canineeye@purdue.edu
www.vet.purdue.edu/yshen/cerf

Deafness

Dr. George M. Strain, PhD
Department of Comparative Biomedical
    Science
School of Veterinary Medicine
Louisiana State University
Baton Rouge LA 70803
(225) 578-9758
FAX: (225) 578-9895
strain@lsu.edu

DNA

Celera AgGen
Celera Genomics–Rockville
45 West Guide Dr
Rockville MD 20850
(240) 453-3000
FAX: (240) 453-4000
www.celera.com

DNA

The Deubler Genetic Disease Testing Lab
University of Pennsylvania
(888) 736-6436
(215) 898-3375
FAX: (215) 573-2162
penngen@vet.upenn.edu
www.vet.upenn.edu/facultyanddepartments

DNA

OptiGen, LLC
Cornell Business & Technology Park
767 Warren Rd, Ste 300
Ithaca NY 14850
(607) 257-0301
FAX: (607) 257-0353
genetest@optigen.com

DNA

Stormont Laboratories
1237 E. Beamer St, Ste D
Woodland CA 95776
(530) 661-3078
FAX: (530) 661-0391
stormont@stormont-labs.com
www.stormont-labs.com

DNA
VetGen Canine Genetic Services
3728 Plaza Dr, Ste 1
Ann Arbor MI 48108
(800) 483-8436
(734) 669-8440
FAX: (734) 669-8441
vetgen@vetgen.com
www.vetgen.com

Epilepsy
Dr. Gary Johnson
Department of Veterinary Pathology
College of Veterinary Medicine
University of Missouri
209A Connaway Hall
Columbia MO 65211
(573) 884-3712
FAX: (573) 884-5414

Genetic Disease Control (GDC)
Institute for Genetic Disease Control
    in Animals
PO Box 177
Warner NH 03278
(603) 456-2350
(877) 741-2155
gdc@conknet.com
www.vetmed.ucdavis.edu/gdc/gdc.html

Genetic Skin Diseases
Genodermatosis Research Foundation (GRF)
3818 22nd St NW
Canton OH 44708

Hip Dysplasia
Orthopedic Foundation for Animals (OFA)
Dr. Greg Keller, Executive Director
2300 E. Nifong Blvd
Columbia MO 65201-3856
(573) 442-0418
FAX: (573) 875-5073
ofa@offa.org
www.offa.org

Hip Dysplasia
PennHIP
University of Pennsylvania
3900 Delancey St
Philadelphia PA 10104-6010
(215) 573-3176
pennhipinfo@pennhip.org
www.pennhip.org

Metabolism
Screening Lab for Inborn Errors of Metabolism
Section of Medical Genetics
School of Veterinary Medicine
University of Pennsylvania
3900 Delancey St
Philadelphia PA 19104-6010
(215) 898-8894
FAX: (215) 573-2162
penngen@vet.upenn.edu
www.vet.upenn.edu/research/centers/penngen

Mouth Problems
Dr. Edward Eisner, DVM
Tendercare Veterinary Medical Center
5930 South Holly St
Greenwood Village CO 80111
(303) 759-4728
FAX: (303) 689-9102
www.tendercarevet.com
www.denvervetdental.com

Poison Control
ASPCA Animal Poison Control.Center
College of Veterinary Medicine
University of Illinois
2001 S. Lincoln Ave
Urbana IL 61801
(888) 426-4435
napcc@aspca.org
(for general non-emergency information)
www.aspca.org

Progressive Retinal Atrophy (PRA)

James A. Baker Institute for Animal Health
College of Veterinary Medicine
Cornell University
Hungerford Hill Rd
Ithaca NY 14853-6401
(607) 256-5600
FAX: (607) 256-5608
Baker_Institute@cornell.edu
www.bakerinstitute.vet.cornell.edu

Thyroid

Endocrine Diagnostic Section
Animal Health Diagnostic Laboratory
College of Veterinary Medicine
Michigan State University
PO Box 30078
Lansing MI 48909-7576
(517) 353-0621
www.ahdl.msu.edu
(check for special shipping requirements)

Thyroid

Diagnostic Laboratory
NY State College of Veterinary Medicine
Cornell University
PO Box 5786
Ithaca NY 14853-5786
(607) 253-3900
FAX: (607) 253-3949
diaglab@cornell.edu

To transport dogs to other countries, especially to Australia, the following labs can be helpful:

Brucellosis

National Veterinary Services Laboratories
1800 Dayton Rd
Ames IA 50010
(515) 239-8266
www.aphis.usda.gov/vs

Ehrlichia Canis

Immofluorescent Antibody Test
Oklahoma Animal Disease Diagnostic
    Laboratory
Oklahoma State University
PO Box 7001
Stillwater OK 74076-7001
(405) 744-6623
FAX: (405) 744-8612
oaddl@cvm.okstate.edu

Leptospirosis

Texas Veterinary Medical Diagnostic
    Laboratory
Drawer 3040
College Station TX 77841-3040
(888) 646-5623
(979) 845-3414
FAX: (979) 845-1794
www.tvmdlweb.tamu.edu

Rabies Anitbody Titer

Rapid Fluorescent Focus Inhibition Test
Rabies Laboratory/RFFIT
Mosier Hall
Kansas State University
1800 Denison Ave
Manhattan KS 66506-5600
(785) 532-4483
FAX: (785) 532-4474
rabies@vet.k-state.edu
www.vet.ksu.edu/depts/rabies/index.htm

Vet articles can be purchased through *iknowledge.com*

Douglas Novick, DVM, President
4820 Croy Rd
Morgan Hill CA 95037
(408) 779-6776
dnovick@iknowledgenow.com
info@iknowledgenow.com
www.iknowledgenow.com
subscriptions@salesiknowledge.com

RECOMMENDED READING AND OTHER MEDIA

The Complete Dog Book, 19th edition, American Kennel Club, Howell Book House, 1998.

Another Piece of the Puzzle: Puppy Development, Pat Hastings and Erin Ann Rouse, editors, Dogfolk Enterprises, 2004. Call (800) 967-3188 or log on to www.dogfolk.com to order this book.

"Better Breeding Column," AKC Gazette, Pat Craige Trotter and Cindy Vogels.

Bites, Breath & Benevolent Breeding, Edward Eisner DVM, 5th edition, 2005. Call (303) 759-4728 or visit www.denvervetdental.com.

Born to Win, Patricia Craig, Doral Publishing, 1997.

Canine Reproduction - A Breeder's Guide, Dr. Phyllis A. Holst, Alpine Publications, 1985.

Canine Terminology, Harold Spira, Howell Book House, 1982. Available through www.dogfolk.com and www.dogwise.com.

"The Doberman Pinscher CD," Sherluck Multimedia, 1996. Call (253) 631-1442 or email sherluckmm@msn.com (CDs on other breeds are also available from Sherluck Multimedia.)

The Dog in Action, McDowell Lyon, Howell Book House, 1950.

Dog Locomotion and Gait Analysis, Curtis M. Brown, Hoflin Publications, 1986.

Dog Steps, Rachel Page Elliott, Howell Book House, 1973. This is both a book and a video.

K-9 Structure & Terminology, Edward M. Gilbert Jr. and Thlema Brown, Dogfolk Enterprises, 2001. Call (800) 967-3188 or log on to www.dogfolk.com to order this book.

"Puppy Puzzle: The Hastings Approach to Evaluating the Structural Quality of Puppies," Bob and Pat Hastings and Erin Rouse, Dogfolk Enterprises, 1998. Call (800) 967-3188 or log on to www.dogfolk.com to order this video.

Solving the Mysteries of Breed Type, Richard Beauchamp, Doral Publishing, 2002.

Successful Dog Breeding, Chris Walkowicz and Bonnie Wilcox DVM, Prentice Hall Press, 1987.

UC Davis School of Veterinary Medicine Book of Dogs, Harper Collins Publishers, 1995.

table of visuals

index

Pat Hastings has been involved in the dog world since 1959. She started her career as an owner-handler and then moved on to breeding and professional handling with her late husband, E.R. "Bob" Hastings. She is currently an AKC judge and a highly respected educator in the dog world. Her articles have appeared in such publications as the *AKC Gazette*, *Dog News*, *Clean Run* and numerous breed magazines. Her seminars, presentations and litter evaluations have benefited fanciers for over 15 years.

In 1998, she founded Dogfolk Enterprises to contribute to the education of breeders, owners, handlers and judges with products such as her best-selling instructional video, "Puppy Puzzle: The Hastings Approach to Evaluating the Structural Quality of Puppies," and the popular book, *Another Piece of the Puzzle: Puppy Development*, edited by Pat Hastings and Erin Ann Rouse.

Erin Ann Rouse has been writing and editing professionally for over 25 years and has collaborated with Pat Hastings since 1995. Their series, "Dog Shows 101," printed in *Dog Nose News*, won the 2002 Dog Writers Association award for best magazine series. Her articles have also appeared in such publications as *Doberman World* and *Choban Chatter*.

THE PUPPY PUZZLE VIDEO IS GOING DVD!!!

This classic is soon to be released in DVD format and will include new features that expand on the original information.

Find out more about shoulders, knees, topline issues, front angles, rear angles and many other elements of structure. The DVD will also provide an introduction to Structure in Action.

Puppy Puzzle DVD Coming Soon to a DVD Player Near You!

DOGFOLK
ENTERPRISES

Lead off with dogfolk.com

be part of the experience!

Pat Hastings' PUPPY PUZZLE PRESENTATION

This presentation is based on Pat Hastings' acclaimed video,
**PUPPY PUZZLE: THE HASTINGS APPROACH TO EVALUATING
THE STRUCTURAL QUALITY OF PUPPIES**, and offers information that
can benefit everyone working with dogs and every puppy out of a serious
breeding program.

The single most important decision we can make for our puppies is to determine
whether they are structurally sound enough to do what we will ask of them in
their lifetimes. Whether our goal is the show ring and whelping box,
performance competitions, working trials or services for independence, we owe it
to our dogs to know in which lifestyle each may best flourish.
This presentation is held primarily at National Specialties.

**Check the Dogfolk website
for more information and for
scheduled presentations.**

DOGFOLK
ENTERPRISES

Lead off with dogfolk.com

behind every great dog is a conscientious person

In her **PUPPY PUZZLE** video, Pat Hastings discusses the importance of evaluating the inborn structural quality of puppies.

In **ANOTHER PIECE OF THE PUZZLE: PUPPY DEVELOPMENT**, the focus is on the effective nurturing of puppies' physical, mental and emotional growth.

ANOTHER PIECE OF THE PUZZLE strives, through selected writings by experienced dog people, to illuminate the many ways that humans can increase their puppies' potential for a wonderful life. From a synopsis of scientific research to effective whelping and rearing practices, this book celebrates the human-canine bond of the 21st century.

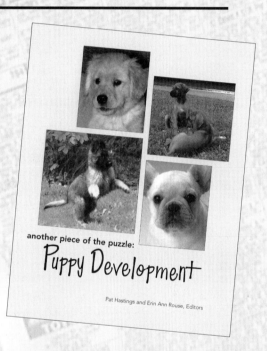

another piece of the puzzle:

Puppy Development

Pat Hastings and Erin Ann Rouse, Editors

"Whether you're a breeder, exhibitor, performance competitor, puppy owner or prospective puppy buyer, we encourage you to read all sections of this book. What you learn may surprise you or at least make you better prepared for your next experience with puppies."

— Pat Hastings and Erin Ann Rouse, editors

DOGFOLK
ENTERPRISES

Lead off with dogfolk.com

Check out our Group Winners.

K-9 STRUCTURE & TERMINOLOGY, by Ed Gilbert and Thelma Brown: This classic provides a comprehensive text on the canine physique . . . and its associated lexicon.

The best-selling **PUPPY PUZZLE** video: Pat Hastings discusses how to evaluate the structural quality of puppies effectively . . . and why.

These greats and more are available on dogfolk.com

From educational services to recommended show-dog products, dogfolk.com can help you get where you want to be in the dog world.

DOGFOLK
ENTERPRISES

Lead off with dogfolk.com